science for a changing world

Climate and Land Use Change Research and Development Program

Development of a Numerical Model to Simulate Groundwater Flow in the Shallow Aquifer System of Assateague Island, Maryland and Virginia

By John P. Masterson, Michael N. Fienen, Dean B. Gesch, and Carl S. Carlson

Open-File Report 2013–1111

U.S. Department of the Interior
U.S. Geological Survey

U.S. Department of the Interior
SALLY JEWELL, Secretary

U.S. Geological Survey
Suzette M. Kimball, Acting Director

U.S. Geological Survey, Reston, Virginia: 2013

For more information on the USGS—the Federal source for science about the Earth, its natural and living resources, natural hazards, and the environment—visit *http://www.usgs.gov* or call 1–888–ASK–USGS

For an overview of USGS information products, including maps, imagery, and publications, visit *http://www.usgs.gov/pubprod*

To order this and other USGS information products, visit *http://store.usgs.gov*

Contents

Figures

Tables

Conversion Factors, Datum, and Abbreviations

Inch/Pound to SI

Multiply	By	To obtain
Length		
inch (in.)	2.54	centimeter (cm)
inch (in.)	25.4	millimeter (mm)
foot (ft)	0.3048	meter (m)
mile (mi)	1.609	kilometer (km)
Area		
square foot (ft^2)	929.0	square centimeter (cm^2)
square foot (ft^2)	0.09290	square meter (m^2)
square inch (in^2)	6.452	square centimeter (cm^2)
square mile (mi^2)	2.590	square kilometer (km^2)
Volume		
gallon (gal)	3.785	liter (L)
gallon (gal)	0.003785	cubic meter (m^3)
million gallons (Mgal)	3,785	cubic meter (m^3)
cubic inch (in^3)	16.39	cubic centimeter (cm^3)
cubic inch (in^3)	0.01639	cubic decimeter (dm^3)
cubic inch (in^3)	0.01639	liter (L)
cubic foot (ft^3)	0.02832	cubic meter (m^3)
Flow rate		
foot per second (ft/s)	0.3048	meter per second (m/s)
foot per day (ft/d)	0.3048	meter per day (m/d)
foot per year (ft/yr)	0.3048	meter per year (m/yr)
cubic foot per second (ft^3/s)	0.02832	cubic meter per second (m^3/s)
million gallons per day (Mgal/d)	0.04381	cubic meter per second (m^3/s)
inch per year (in/yr)	25.4	millimeter per year (mm/yr)
Density		
pound per cubic foot (lb/ft^3)	16.02	kilogram per cubic meter (kg/m^3)
pound per cubic foot (lb/ft^3)	0.01602	gram per cubic centimeter (g/cm^3)
Hydraulic conductivity		
foot per day (ft/d)	0.3048	meter per day (m/d)
Hydraulic gradient		
foot per mile (ft/mi)	0.1894	meter per kilometer (m/km)

Transmissivity*		
foot squared per day (ft^2/d)	0.09290	meter squared per day (m^2/d)
Leakance		
foot per day per foot [(ft/d)/ft]	1	meter per day per meter
inch per year per foot [(in/yr)/ft]	83.33	millimeter per year per meter [(mm/yr)/m]

Temperature in degrees Celsius (°C) may be converted to degrees Fahrenheit (°F) as follows: °F=(1.8×°C)+32

Temperature in degrees Fahrenheit (°F) may be converted to degrees Celsius (°C) as follows: °C=(°F-32)/1.8

Vertical coordinate information is referenced to North American Vertical Datum of 1988 (NAVD 88).

Horizontal coordinate information is referenced to the North American Datum of 1983 (NAD 83).

Altitude, as used in this report, refers to distance above the vertical datum.

* Specific conductance is given in microsiemens per centimeter at 25 degrees Celsius (µS/cm at 25 °C).

Concentrations of chemical constituents in water are given either in grams per liter (g/L) or parts per thousand (ppt).

Abbreviations

bls	below land surface
EAARL	Experimental Advanced Airborne Research LiDAR
EMI	electromagnetic induction
MHW	mean high water
NOAA	National Oceanic and Atmospheric Administration
USGS	U.S. Geological Survey
ppt	parts per thousand

Development of a Numerical Model to Simulate Groundwater Flow in the Shallow Aquifer System of Assateague Island, Maryland and Virginia

By John P. Masterson, Michael N. Fienen, Dean Gesch, and Carl S. Carlson

Abstract

A three-dimensional groundwater-flow model was developed for Assateague Island in eastern Maryland and Virginia to simulate both groundwater flow and solute (salt) transport to evaluate the groundwater system response to sea-level rise. The model was constructed using geologic and spatial information to represent the island geometry, boundaries, and physical properties and was calibrated using an inverse modeling parameter-estimation technique. An initial transient solute-transport simulation was used to establish the freshwater-saltwater boundary for a final calibrated steady-state model of groundwater flow. This model was developed as part of an ongoing investigation by the U.S. Geological Survey Climate and Land Use Change Research and Development Program to improve capabilities for predicting potential climate-change effects and provide the necessary tools for adaptation and mitigation of potentially adverse impacts.

Introduction

Assateague Island lies along the Atlantic coast of Maryland and Virginia (fig. 1). It is an undeveloped barrier island complex backed by wetland and marsh systems and consists of large stretches of dunes separated by low-lying areas that often are submerged or overwashed during storm surges. This barrier island complex is characterized by low topographic relief with a mean altitude of about 2 meters (m) and maximum dune altitudes of about 15 m above mean sea level (as defined by the North American Vertical Datum of 1988). The effects of climate change and sea-level rise on this barrier island complex are expected to include changes in erosion rates, island morphology, marsh health, and groundwater flow. These changes will affect use of the island by both humans and wildlife; specifically, the island serves as an important breeding ground and habitat for endangered species, such as piping plovers. In response to these concerns, the U.S. Geological Survey (USGS) is working with State and other Federal agencies to improve the understanding of potential climate-change effects on coastal ecosystems, including the effects on groundwater flow. These efforts include developing capabilities for predicting climate-change effects, and to provide the necessary tools for adaptation to and mitigation of potentially adverse impacts.

The study area is underlain by unconsolidated sediments that form a wedge of sands, silts, and clays over 2 kilometers (km) thick. These sediments compose a series of confined and unconfined aquifers collectively known as the Northern Atlantic Coastal Plain aquifer system (Trapp and Horn, 1997). The regional confined aquifer system is generally overlain by younger sediments ranging in age from Tertiary to Quaternary in the study area. These sediments were deposited in a variety of environments, including alluvial, tidal marsh, back barrier, and marine marginal, and form an unconfined, surficial aquifer. The groundwater hydrology of Assateague Island is controlled largely by the landforms of the island (Krantz, 2009).

The water table in the shallow, unconfined aquifer system generally follows the local topography, and water levels can range from land surface to as deep as 15 m below land surface (bls). However, the water table often is less than 1 m bls (Dillow and others, 2002). The only surface-water features on the island are a limited number of groundwater-fed ponds, which represent surface-water expressions of the water table. As a result, the groundwater hydrology, including the distribution of fresh and brackish water in the shallow aquifer, and the geometry of the fresh groundwater lens beneath the island affects the distribution of plant communities and habitat for a diverse community of invertebrate and vertebrate wildlife (Krantz, 2009).

The areas within Assateague Island that are considered to be most vulnerable to sea-level rise are those with the highest occurrence of overwash and the highest rates of shoreline change (Pendleton and others, 2004). However, in addition to increased erosion and surface inundation from rising sea level, the groundwater-flow system can be substantially affected by increased water-table altitude, subsurface flooding of low-lying areas, and the potential for saltwater intrusion (Masterson and Garabedian, 2007). Understanding how sea-level rise may affect groundwater hydrology in shallow, unconfined coastal systems such as Assateague Island may be vital for assessing the potential impacts of sea-level rise on the sustainability of Federally listed endangered species, such as piping plovers. This information is not currently available to resource managers and decision makers at Assateague Island National Seashore.

A numerical model of groundwater flow was developed to represent freshwater and saltwater flow in the shallow barrier-island groundwater-flow system beneath Assateague Island. The purpose of this analysis was to determine the effects of increased sea-level altitude on water levels (depth to the water table) and the position of the freshwater-saltwater interface in this shallow groundwater-flow system. This effort was initiated and supported by the U.S. Geological Survey (USGS) Climate and Land Use Change Research and Development Program.

The purpose of this report is to document the development of the numerical model used in this investigation. A detailed description of the parameter-estimation techniques used to calibrate this model is included in the report. This description includes the initial and optimal parameter values and measured and model-calculated water levels and salinity concentrations.

Development of a Numerical Model

Numerical models provide a means to synthesize existing hydrogeologic information into an internally consistent mathematical representation of a real system or process and, thus, are useful tools for testing and improving conceptual models or hypotheses of groundwater-flow systems (Konikow and Reilly, 1999). A three-dimensional groundwater-flow and solute-transport model was developed for the groundwater-flow system beneath Assateague Island. This numerical model is based on the USGS computer program SEAWAT2000 (Langevin and others, 2007) that can simulate variable-density and time-varying groundwater flow. SEAWAT2000 is a computer code that combines the groundwater-flow code MODFLOW–2000 (Harbaugh and others, 2000) with the solute transport capabilities of MT3D (Zheng and Wang, 1999), thus allowing fluid density to vary according to solute (salt) concentration. The purpose of this numerical model is to (1) simulate current conditions of groundwater flow on Assateague, (2) better understand interaction between freshwater- and saltwater-flow systems, and (3) assess potential long-term effects of sea-level rise on the freshwater-flow system beneath Assateague Island.

The distribution of aquifer characteristics incorporated into the model was derived from available hydrologic data and geologic descriptions (Owens and Denny, 1979; Morton and others, 2007; Krantz, 2009; Krantz and others, 2009). The model then was calibrated to groundwater levels and electromagnetic induction (EMI) logs measured in October 2010 using the parameter estimation (PEST) software suite (Doherty, 2010).

Model Discretization

The finite-difference model grid consists of a series of orthogonal model cells in which user-specified hydraulic parameters, model stresses, and boundary conditions are varied spatially. The conceptualization of how and where water enters, moves through, and leaves the aquifer is critical to the development of an accurate flow model (Reilly, 2001). Model inputs include intrinsic aquifer characteristics in each model cell, such as hydraulic conductivity. Boundary conditions are applied at some model cells to simulate hydrologic features, including the saline surface-water bodies that surround Assateague Island. A detailed discussion of grid discretization, boundary conditions, and the use of finite-difference equations to simulate groundwater flow is presented in McDonald and Harbaugh (1988).

Spatial Discretization

The model developed of the Assateague Island groundwater-flow system required a numerical grid with a resolution necessary to represent both small topographic variations in the horizontal dimension and the transition zone between freshwater and saltwater in the vertical dimension, but the model was balanced by the need to work within current computational limitations. The finite-difference grid for the numerical model consists of uniformly spaced model cells that are 50 m on a side. The grid consists of 1,240 rows and 300 columns and extends south from the Ocean City Inlet in Maryland to Toms Cove, Virginia (fig. 2). The model grid includes the mainland area west of Sinepuxent and Chincoteague Bays; however, the active model area was limited to an area surrounding the barrier island of about 3,000 m west into Chincoteague Bay and about 1,500 to 2,500 m east into the Atlantic Ocean. Sinepuxent Neck in the northern part of the study area was included in the analysis because of the potential for underflow from the mainland beneath Sinepuxent Bay (fig. 2). In this area, Ayers Creek (fig. 1) is the westernmost boundary extent.

The model has 10 layers that extend from land surface to a maximum depth of 30 m below the North American Vertical Datum of 1988 (NAVD 88) with vertical layering ranging from 0.5 to 12 m in thickness (fig. 3). Median land-surface altitudes and bathymetric depths for each model cell were used to define the uppermost active layer in a particular row and column (fig. 4). The merged topographic-bathymetric elevation data were developed from several data sources at a grid spacing of 1/9-arc-second (approximately 3 m) in a geographic (latitude/longitude) coordinate system. The source data for the Assateague Island topography was a 2-meter digital elevation model derived from lidar (Light Detection and Ranging) data collected in 2008 using the Experimental Advanced Airborne Research lidar (EAARL) instrument (Nayegandhi and others, 2009). The bathymetric data on the ocean side of the island were derived from the National Oceanic and Atmospheric Administration (NOAA) hydrographic survey data, and the bay side bathymetric data came from hydrographic surveys conducted for the State of Maryland and the National Park Service in 2000, 2003, and 2007. The topographic-bathymetric dataset was resampled and projected to a grid spacing of 25 m on a side.

The model represents the full thickness of the shallow groundwater system, extending from the water table to the top of the Upper Chesapeake confining unit (shown as the Yorktown and Eastover Formations (undivided) on fig. 5); layer thicknesses vary vertically and generally are based on the geometry of hydrogeologic units and the need for increased vertical discretization in the shallow part of the system to minimize numerical dispersion issues as part of the numerical simulations. Overall, the grid contains 3,720,000 cells, of which fewer than half (1,659,780) are used to represent the active part of the flow system.

Temporal Discretization

The final calibrated model described in this report is a steady-state model. However, a transient model was used first to establish the freshwater-saltwater interface boundary condition for the steady-state model. The stress periods simulated in this transient model varied depending upon the analysis. A long initial period of about 1,000 years was simulated as part of the model calibration process to solve for the position and movement of the freshwater-saltwater interface and to provide a best fit of model-calculated water levels to the measured data.

Hydrologic Boundary Conditions

The hydrologic boundaries, or boundary conditions, in the groundwater-flow model are the areas from which, and the method by which, all the water entering and leaving the model is specified. The boundaries of the numerical model of fresh groundwater flow in the Assateague Island groundwater-flow system were designed to coincide with the physical boundaries of the flow system. In this analysis both freshwater- and saltwater-flow systems were simulated to determine the boundary between the fresh and salt groundwater-flow systems. The lower and lateral boundaries of the freshwater-flow system are the transition areas between freshwater and saltwater, which were calculated by the numerical model. There were no anthropogenic stresses (i.e. pumping wells) simulated in this model.

Upper Boundary

The active model area in this study includes both land and areas of open water in the Atlantic Ocean and Chincoteague and Sinepuxent Bays; therefore, the upper boundary of the groundwater-flow system consists of the water table and seepage faces on land and the surrounding saline surface-water bodies offshore. The water table is a free surface that fluctuates in response to spatially variable recharge from precipitation that is simulated as a specified flux into the system and from groundwater evapotranspiration from the water table that is simulated as a head-dependent flux boundary condition removing water from the system. Seepage faces were simulated to account for the condition under future rates of sea-level rise when the water table may intersect land surface. This condition was accounted for by head-dependent flux boundaries assigned at every model cell above sea level similar to previous studies on the Delmarva Peninsula (Sanford and others, 2012). The surrounding saline surface-water bodies were represented in this analysis as specified-head–specified-concentration boundaries whose concentrations varied depending on the salinity of the Atlantic Ocean and Chincoteague and Sinepuxent Bays.

Recharge and Groundwater Evapotranspiration

The primary source of recharge on Assateague Island is precipitation. Long-term average precipitation for this area is about 120 centimeters per year (cm/yr) measured at Snow Hill, Maryland, from 1969 to 2009 (National Oceanic and Atmospheric Administration, 2010a). Recharge from precipitation is simulated for four zones (fig. 6) that are labeled A through D and represent increasing rates of infiltration to the water table. The zones were assigned according to substrate and land cover (Krantz, 2009; Morton and others, 2007). These initial rates were consistent with rates from previous analyses of the nearby Eastern Shore area of Virginia (Sanford and others, 2009) and for similar barrier-island settings at Hatteras Island, North Carolina (Anderson and others, 2000), and Fire Island, New York. (Schubert, 2010). The final recharge rates used in the simulation were adjusted slightly as part of the model calibration process, described in the section "Model Calibration." The initial rates of recharge applied to the four model zones were specified as follows: wetlands, 10 cm/yr; grass/scrubs, 20 cm/yr; forested, 40 cm/yr; and unvegetated, 60 cm/yr.

Evapotranspiration (ET) from the water table (groundwater ET) also was considered in the development of this model because of the relatively shallow depth to the water table throughout the island, especially in the low-lying coastal areas along the bay side of the island. Groundwater ET was simulated in the model by assigning a maximum ET flux when the water table is at the land surface and an extinction depth below which the ET flux becomes zero. The ET flux decreases linearly with a decrease in water-table altitude between the specified land surface and ET extinction depths.

The maximum ET flux was specified for every land cell in the top layer, and the water-table altitude was calculated by the model. The maximum ET flux uniformly assigned to each model cell was about 64 cm/yr, which is consistent with previous estimates for this area (Sanford and others, 2009) and is based on earlier estimates of ET rates for the mid-Atlantic region (Milly, 1994).

The land-surface altitude for each model cell was derived from lidar data collected in 2008 by the Experimental Advanced Airborne Research Lidar (EAARL) instrument (Nayegandhi and others, 2009). The extinction depth was determined on the basis of estimates of average root zone depths and was distributed throughout the modeled area by the vegetation coverage used to assign recharge rates (fig. 6). The extinction depths for the forests, shrubs/grasses, and wetland areas were set to 200, 20, and 10 cm, respectively (Sanford and others, 2009, 2012).

Surface Seepage

The model described in this report was developed to assess the effects of sea-level rise on the groundwater-flow system. It is understood that as sea-level rises, the water table in shallow coastal aquifer systems also will rise, and depending on the thickness of the vadose zone, the water table may intersect land surface (Masterson and Garabedian, 2007). To account for this condition, head-dependent flux boundaries in the Drain (DRN) package in SEAWAT (Langevin and others, 2007) were assigned to every model cell above sea level with the stage height specified at the land-surface altitude of each cell (Sanford and others, 2012). These DRN cells remove water from the groundwater system when the water table intersects land surface, thus preventing the water table from rising above the land surface. This method does not provide for the development of new surface-water bodies but does allow for a more physically realistic analysis of the response of the underlying freshwater-saltwater interface in response to a changing sea-level position because it is the altitude of the water table (or surface-water expressions of the water table) above local sea level that generally determines the depth to the underlying freshwater-saltwater interface (Masterson and Garabedian, 2007; Werner and Simmons, 2009).

Saline Surface-Water Bodies

The remaining upper boundary of the flow system consists of the saline surface-water bodies that surround Assateague Island. These surface waters are represented as specified-head–specified-concentration boundaries that vary spatially on the basis of distance from shore on the Atlantic Ocean side and distance from ocean on the bay side of the island. The specified concentrations of salt also varied depending on whether the water bodies were ocean or bay. It was assumed for this analysis that the salt concentrations of the Atlantic Ocean and Chincoteague and Sinepuxent Bays were constant and increased from the bays to the ocean from 29 to 35 grams/liter (Wells and others, 1999; Bratton and others, 2009). The decreased salinity in the back-barrier bays is a result of freshwater discharge to these bays from the mainland.

The specified-head values assigned to these boundaries were for mean high water (MHW) relative to NAVD 88 and were determined using VDatum, the National Oceanic and Atmospheric Administration's National Geodetic Survey vertical datum transformation program (Parker and others, 2003). The interpolated heads varied spatially depending on distance from the shore on the Atlantic Ocean side of the island and distance from the Toms Cove and Ocean City Inlets on the bay side of the island (fig. 7).

Additional altitude was added to the nearshore areas along the ocean side of the island to account for the effects of wave runup and tidal pumping, each of which can elevate the nearshore water table at this boundary creating a local mounding of the water table commonly referred to as water-table overheight (Nielsen, 1999; Nielsen and Hanslow, 1991). A value of 1.16 m above NAVD 88 was calculated for the water-table overheight for this analysis, which is consistent with the analysis conducted by Schubert (2010) for a similar barrier island setting on Fire Island, N.Y. The specified-head value assigned to the offshore areas of the Atlantic Ocean beyond the nearshore wave influence was 0.16 m, which was based on the current sea-level altitude recorded at the Ocean City, Maryland, tidal gauge (fig. 8; National Oceanic and Atmospheric Administration, 2010b).

Lateral and Lower Model Boundaries

The lower boundary of the freshwater-flow system is the transition between freshwater and saltwater, which is calculated by the numerical model as part of this analysis. The arbitrary bottom altitude of 30 m below NAVD 88 was specified as a no-flow boundary for this analysis; this altitude generally coincides with the top of the Upper Chesapeake confining unit (not shown), which separates the surficial aquifers from the uppermost confined aquifer in the Northern Atlantic Coastal Plain deposits (Trapp and Horn, 1997). This lower no-flow boundary is sufficiently deep that it does not affect the model-calculated position and movement of the freshwater-saltwater interface beneath the shallow flow system beneath Assateague Island.

The lateral and lower boundaries were, for the most part, simulated as no-flow boundary conditions selected to extend beyond the maximum limit of the freshwater-flow system. The exceptions to this were the lateral boundary in the northern part of the study area on Sinepuxent Neck and in the lower layers along the western boundary beneath Chincoteague Bay (fig. 2). Along Ayers Creek on Sinepuxent Neck a specified-head boundary was assigned to the western edge of the model to account for flow entering from the west from the mainland.

For the length of the western edge of the model beneath Chincoteague Bay, it was assumed that freshwater flow from the mainland did not extend beneath Chincoteague Bay to Assateague Island in the surficial deposits of the Coastal Plain sediments (model layers 1–7). However, it was assumed that beneath the Upper Chesapeake confining unit, the potential exists for subsea discharge beyond the eastern extent of Assateague Island; therefore, a specified-flux boundary condition was assigned to the western edge of the active model area in layers 8–10 to account for any potential underflow from the confined Northern Atlantic Coastal Plain aquifers beneath Chincoteague Bay.

The specified-flux boundary condition was simulated by the WEL package in SEAWAT, and the inflow rate specified in each model cell was calculated using the Darcy flux determined by the flow from the constant heads specified in the northern part of the study area near Sinepuxent Neck. The specified-flux boundary was selected instead of the specified-head boundary used along the western boundary near Sinepuxent Neck to avoid a potential problem with salt dispersion into the aquifer because of the strong salt concentration gradient where fresher groundwater discharges into more saline water (Mulligan and others, 2011). This was not of concern near Sinepuxent Neck because the freshwater specified-head cells were in the freshwater-flow system in the northern part of the study area.

Initial Conditions

To simulate both freshwater and saltwater flow, an initial estimate of the transition zone between freshwater and saltwater must be assumed. The better the estimate of the position of the freshwater-saltwater interface, the less simulation time required to achieve a final, stable solution of the interface position (Langevin and others, 2007). The initial estimate of the interface in this analysis was assumed to be parallel to the island shoreline extending to a uniform depth of about 10 m below NAVD88. The simulation of flow and solute transport with SEAWAT (Langevin and others, 2007) requires transient conditions to establish the freshwater-saltwater interface for future simulations. Transient simulations were made from the initial salt concentration until a reasonable approximation of the freshwater-saltwater interface was achieved and the model had reached a quasi-steady-state condition with respect to simulated hydrologic conditions. This solution was used as the initial conditions for subsequent analyses of sea-level rise through 2100 (not presented in this report).

The simulation of solute transport was made using an implicit finite-difference solution with advective transport only (Langevin and others, 2007) to calculate the position and movement of the transition zone between freshwater and saltwater. This solution was necessary for the size of the model domain in this analysis, but results in larger numerical dispersion or smearing of the simulated transition zone between freshwater and saltwater. The resulting numerical dispersion from these simulations is similar in magnitude to the observed transition zone from the EMI logs for current conditions (generally less than 5 m thick).

Hydraulic Properties

The hydraulic properties requirements for the numerical model developed for this analysis include horizontal hydraulic conductivity (kx), vertical hydraulic conductivity (kz), porosity, specific yield, and storage coefficient. The determination of these hydraulic properties is based largely on the limited hydrogeologic information available for Assateague Island, on the relation between the geologic framework and aquifer properties determined from previous analyses in similar hydrogeologic settings (Dillow and others, 2002; Krantz, 2009; Krantz and others, 2009; Schubert, 2010; fig. 5), and on hydrogeologic information obtained from a network of 13 monitoring-well pairs installed along 5 transects (fig. 8) (Banks and others, 2012). In addition to water levels, gamma and EMI logs were measured at these well sites to characterize the lithology and to monitor the current depth of the freshwater-saltwater interface in the shallow groundwater system that underlies Assateague Island.

The initial hydraulic-property values distributed throughout the modeled area were consistent with those of a flow-modeling analysis in a similar setting on Fire Island, N.Y. (Schubert, 2010). Specific yield for layer 1 was set to a value of 0.2, specific storage value for layers 2– 10 was $1.0 \times 10e^{-04}$, and uniform porosity value of 0.3 was set for the entire model domain. These initial values were not varied as part of the calibration process. The initial estimates of hydraulic conductivity, however, were adjusted using an inverse model-calibration technique (Doherty, 2010; Doherty and Hunt, 2010) to adjust the parameter values until a subjective best fit was obtained between the observed and model-calculated water levels. A more detailed description of the calibration process and the final hydraulic properties simulated in the flow model can be found in the following section on "Model Calibration."

Model Calibration

Calibration of the Assateague Island model was based on head observations and salinity measurements made on October 3–5, 2010. The calibration process was performed in multiple steps. These steps, outlined broadly, were (1) assembling available data, (2) assigning weights to data, (3) defining hydraulic parameterization (discretization and zoning), (4) conducting manual "trial-and-error" calibration to determine initial parameter values, (5) conducting sensitivity analysis, (6) iteratively exchanging parameter values between parameter estimation steps, and (7) revising the conceptual model and observation weights. These steps do not necessarily follow in sequence from one to the other because feedbacks throughout the process identify shortcomings and indicate changes that cascade throughout the process. The final calibrated model is based on the results at each step, so each step is described in this section.

Assembling Available Data

The data available for model calibration in this investigation are based on synoptic measurements of water levels and salinity (measured through borehole EMI logs), as described by Banks and others (2012; figs. 8 and 9). The EMI logs were used to delineate changes in the aquifer materials and (or) changes in electrical properties of porewater (for instance, to identify freshwater or saltwater). In freshwater, clays and silts generally have higher electrical conductivity than sands and gravels. However, if the sand or gravel unit is saturated with a highly conductive fluid, such as brackish water or saltwater, then the conductivity of the coarse material can have a higher conductivity value than that of the fine materials (Williams and others, 1993). Because of this complexity, the gamma and EMI logs were interpreted together to determine whether increased conductivity is likely caused by the presence of clay and silt or by electrically conductive water. In addition, measurements of specific conductance, temperature, and water levels were made in the shallow and deeper wells at each well cluster to help interpret the borehole logs and identify the source of the conductivity. A comparison of the gamma and EMI logs collected at the 13 deep wells in the 5 transects shown in figure 8 provides the information necessary to characterize changes in aquifer material and salinity; the information is needed to determine the extent of the shallow freshwater lens and the presence of a deeper freshwater-flow system underlying Assateague Island.

Barrier islands compose a challenging location at which to determine representative, steady-state conditions from the limited data available because of tides and storm-surge overwash that effect the variability of head and salinity in this dynamic environment. As a result, the conductivity values obtained from the EMI logs (fig. 9) were used only as a qualitative measure to develop a reasonable simulation of the freshwater-saltwater interface position for current (2010) conditions. A more rigorous calibration of the model to salinity data would require more measurements over a longer period of time to assess the effects of overland flooding of saline surface waters on the salinity profiles observed in the shallow part of the groundwater system in order to differentiate transient storm-event driven salinities from long-term ambient conditions.

Water-level measurements were made synoptically in 15 wells during several events from August 2010 to October 2010, and continuous measurements were recorded in 9 wells for multiple months (Banks and others, 2012). The continuous-measurement sites showed water-level trends spanning several weeks and provided information on the aquifer response to several precipitation events that occurred during that period. Given the paucity of water-level data throughout the island, it was determined for this analysis that the relative positions of water-level measurements to one another provide more information on flow directions, hydraulic gradients, and system dynamics than actual head values. For this analysis, water levels measured during the borehole geophyscial logging (October 3–5, 2010) were used for model calibration (table 1).

Weight Assignment for Observation Data

From regression theory, it is ideal for weights to represent the reciprocal of observation uncertainty (Draper and Smith, 1966; Hill and Tiedeman, 2007). Observation uncertainty can also be thought of as epistemic uncertainty (Rubin, 2003), which is made up of measurement error and structural uncertainty resulting from the limits of data availability, well construction, sampling methods, and other factors difficult to quantify that are expected to preclude perfect reproduction of the observation data. Doherty and Welter (2010) and Doherty and Hunt (2010) discuss the important subjective role that observation weights have in the model-calibration process.

The goal of using observation uncertainty for weighting represents an ideal case where such uncertainty is readily quantified. The structural error resulting from factors beyond simply measurement errors is difficult to quantify in practice. Furthermore, issues, including redundant measurements in space or time, can bias which observations play the largest role in informing the parameter-estimation process. Considering all of these factors, the assignment and revision of observation weights takes place throughout the parameter-estimation process. The final optimal weights for the observation data are presented in table 1.

For the final step in the calibration process, epistemic uncertainty of 0.1 m was assigned to most shallow water-level measurements (well name suffix: _S). An exception to this was the value for monitoring well Km09C_S (USGS site 381452075080102). It was determined that the water levels measured at this site were anomalously higher than those of the surrounding wells, possibly the result of issues with the well development, altitude surveying, or locally perched water-table conditions; therefore, water levels measured at this site are considered not representative of ambient conditions (Banks and others, 2012). In this case, a weight of zero was assigned to this observation. By retaining the observation value, but setting the weight to zero, PEST reports the value for inspection, but the value is not considered in the parameter-estimation algorithm. The water-level measurements reported for the deep wells (well name suffix: _D) were also assigned observation weights of zero because the focus of this investigation was on the shallow groundwater system, specifically changes in the vadose-zone thickness in response to sea-level rise. Finally, particular interest in the water levels near the transect at wells Km28 (fig. 8, table 1) provided justification for an increase in the weights for observation data from this location—weight equivalent to epistemic uncertainty of 0.02 m. This qualitative and interpretive calibration step constrains the parameters selected to better reproduce the observation data for the wells along transect Km28 at the expense of matching water levels at the other monitoring wells.

Hydraulic Parameterization by Trial and Error

Using water-level (head) values and salinity concentrations, parameters were adjusted manually through trial and error. Then PEST was used to evaluate the efficacy of the long quasi-steady-state simulation period to achieve a reasonable representation of the freshwater-saltwater interface boundary using the fully coupled flow and transport version of the SEAWAT model. After the approximate location of the freshwater-saltwater interface was reproduced reasonably well by the model, the transport process was disabled in SEAWAT, resulting in a model that considers variable density resulting from salinity concentrations but does not simulate transport of salt through the domain. By doing this, the position of the freshwater-saltwater interface position is set, and the model is only solving for changes in freshwater levels. Freshwater levels generated from this method may differ slightly from those generated with the transport option enabled; however, considering the inherent uncertainty in the limited water-level and salinity calibration data, this step results in much shorter model run times and allows for a much more time-efficient model-calibration process.

Sensitivity Analysis

Following the trial-and-error calibration step, sensitivity analysis was performed to evaluate the sensitivity of the constant heads specified in all 10 layers along the mainland boundary in the extreme northwest of the model (fig. 6A). Little information was available to accurately assign a starting value for this parameter, but sensitivity analysis was performed to confirm that it was an insensitive parameter, and thus could be set at a relatively uncertain starting value with little effect on model performance. Composite-scaled sensitivity, a statistic that summarizes the cumulative amount of information that the observation data contain toward the estimation of a parameter (Hill and Tiedeman, 2007), was calculated for all parameters as part of the sensitivity analysis. The relative composite-scaled sensitivities for all parameters were evaluated at the initial parameter values (fig. 10). As expected, the parameters identified as "sh_l#ml" that represent constant mainland heads for a given model layer (#) showed very low sensitivity. For all future parameter-estimation simulations, these parameter values were set at their initial values. The constant head specified on the bay side in layer 1 (sh_l1b, fig. 10; figs. 2 and 6) was initially estimated and had a high composite-scaled sensitivity, but later was fixed on the basis of the revision of the conceptual model for the Sinepuxent Bay head values discussed below.

One approach to parameter estimation is to set all values with low sensitivity to fixed values. However, in this case, after evaluation of the mainland constant-head boundary values, all of the other parameters in the model were estimated. Stability and uniqueness were achieved using a combination of singular-value decomposition and preferred-value regularization (Doherty and Hunt, 2010).

Revisions to the Conceptual Model and Final Parameter Values

Parameter estimation was conducted in a step-wise manner, and on the basis of the interim results, the conceptual model was revised to improve the fit of simulation results to the observation data. Two main revisions to the conceptual model were performed. The first was to subdivide the hydraulic conductivity in the top three layers along the north-south axis of the island to differentiate between the coarser, more permeable beach sediments on the ocean side of the island from the finer, less permeable sediments on the bay side. The final hydraulic conductivity zonation used in the model is shown in figure 11. The second revision to the initial conceptual model was the adjustment of the constant-head values specified for Sinepuxent and Chincoteague Bays (figs. 2 and 6). The constant-head values were adjusted to account for attenuation of the tidal pulse relative to the ocean side. The initial conceptual model used a single average value for the head in Sinepuxent Bay, but this boundary condition created anomalously high head values in the shallow monitoring wells on the bay side of the island. Measurements of the MHW altitude of sea level obtained from VDatum (fig. 7) were interpolated linearly, and these values were used for the constant-head boundaries along the bay side of the island. The use of values for this boundary condition greatly improved the ability of the model to correctly simulate head values in the shallow monitoring wells along the western shore of the island.

Final optimal parameter values are listed in table 2 and are shown graphically, along with their assumed range or bounds, in figure 12. Most parameter values were optimally estimated within their bounds. This is due, in part, to the use of preferred-value regularization (Doherty and Hunt, 2010). This type of regularization assesses a penalty for deviation of the estimated parameter values from the initial estimates. The result is a tradeoff between model fit and deviation from prior information, a quantitative measure of confidence in initial parameter value. This tradeoff is controlled by the parameter PHIMLIM in PEST (Doherty, 2010). In this analysis, PHIMLIM was set at 15.0 (the number of observations;

Fienen and others, 2009). This setting balances the model fit and deviation from prior information such that the observation weights represent the expected deviation of model-calculated values from measured observation values.

The comparison of model-calculated water levels to estimated water levels included a determination of the mean of the residuals (the difference between estimated and model-calculated water levels) and the absolute mean of the residuals. The absolute mean of the residual was 0.18 m over a range in observations of about 1.4 m. The mean of the residuals (estimated minus model calculated) was -0.02 m, indicating that the residuals have a near random distribution around zero.

The correspondence between measured and model-calculated head values in the monitoring wells used for model calibration are shown in figure 13. The best match is achieved, as expected, in the Km28 transect monitoring wells, which had the highest observation-weight assignments. The matches for the lower-weighted monitoring wells and the zero-weighted monitoring wells were not as good as those for the Km28 transect, but most of the model-calculated water levels in the monitoring wells used for calibration showed improvement in correspondence to the measured values regardless of the observation weight (table 1).

Although the model presents a reasonable match to the observed water-level data, it should be noted that these data only represent water-table conditions for October 3–5, 2010. Given the paucity of hydrologic data available on Assateague Island, it was not possible to determine whether these water-level meaasurements were representative of long-term average conditions. Additional hydrologic data collection would be required to determine average hydrologic conditions for the island, which may then require additional calibration of the groundwater-flow model.

Summary

The U.S. Geological Survey is working with State and other Federal agencies to improve the understanding of climate change on coastal ecosystems, including the effects on groundwater flow; to better develop capabilities for predicting potential climate-change effects; and to provide the necessary tools for adaptation and mitigation of potentially adverse impacts. As part of an ongoing investigation initiated by the U.S. Geological Survey Climate and Land Use Change Research and Development Program, a three-dimensional groundwater-flow model was developed for Assateague Island in eastern Maryland and Virginia to simulate both groundwater flow and salt transport to evaluate the groundwater system response to sea-level rise. The model was constructed using geologic and spatial information to represent the island geometry, boundaries, and physical properties. A lateral grid with a uniform spacing of 50 meters (m) was applied throughout the model. Vertically, the model was subdivided into 10 layers, ranging in thickness from 0.5 m to 12 m to a maximum depth of 30 m below North Atlantic Vertical Datum 1988, the depth to the upper part of the underlying confined Coastal Plain deposits.

The modeled system included specified-head/specified-concentration boundaries representing the saline surface-water bodies. An initial transient solute-transport simulation was used to establish the freshwater-saltwater boundary for a final calibrated steady-state model of groundwater flow. The water table is a free surface that fluctuates in response to spatially variable recharge from precipitation that is simulated as a specified flux to the groundwater system and to groundwater evapotranspiration from the water table simulated as a head-dependent flux boundary condition. A head-dependent flux boundary was specified at the land-surface altitude throughout the model to allow water to discharge at land surface where the water table intersects land surface during the sea-level-rise simulations.

Model calibration was conducted using parameter estimation software and was based on observed water-level and salinity data collected during the field component of this investigation. The model calibration process provided the optimal fitting to the observation data and also allowed for revision of the initial conceptual model of the groundwater system.

References Cited

Anderson, W.P., Evans, D.G., and Snyder, S.W., 2000, The effects of Holocene barrier-island evolution on water-table elevations, Hatteras Island, North Carolina, USA: Hydrogeology Journal, v. 8, no. 4, p. 390–404.

Banks, W.S.L., Masterson, J.P., and Johnson, C.D., 2012, Well network installation and hydrogeologic data collection, Assateague Island National Seashore, Worcester County, Maryland, 2010: U.S. Geological Survey Scientific Investigations Report 2012–5079, 20 p.

Bratton, J.F., Böhlke, J.K., Krantz, D.E., and Tobias, C.R., 2009, Flow and geochemistry of groundwater beneath a back-barrier lagoon: The subterranean estuary at Chincoteague Bay, Maryland, USA: Marine Chemistry, v. 113, p. 78–92.

Dillow, J.J.A., Banks, W.S.L, and Smigaj, M.J., 2002, Groundwater quality and discharge to Chincoteague and Sinepuxent Bays adjacent to Assateague Island National Seashore, Maryland: U.S. Geological Survey Water-Resources Investigations Report 02–4029, 42 p.

Doherty, J.E., and Hunt, R.J., 2010, Approaches to highly parameterized inversion—A guide to using PEST for groundwater-model calibration: U.S. Geological Survey Scientific Investigations Report 2010–5169, 59 p.

Doherty, John, 2010, Model-independent parameter estimation—User manual (5th ed., with slight additions): Brisbane, Australia, Watermark Numerical Computing, 336 p.

Doherty, John and Welter, David, 2010, A short exploration of structural noise: Water Resources Research, v. 46, no. 5, W05525.

Draper, N.R. and Smith, Harry, 1966, Applied regression analysis: New York, Wiley Publishing Co., 407 p.

Fienen, M.N., Muffels, C.T., and Hunt, R.J., 2009, On constraining pilot point calibration with regularization in PEST: Ground Water, v. 47, no. 6, p. 835–844.

Harbaugh, A.W., Banta, E.R., Hill, M.C., and McDonald, M.G., 2000, MODFLOW–2000, the U.S. Geological Survey modular ground-water model—User guide to modularization concepts and the ground-water flow process: U.S. Geological Survey Open-File Report 00–92, 121 p.

Hill, M.C., and Tiedeman, C.R., 2007, Effective groundwater model calibration with analysis of data, sensitivities, predictions, and uncertainty: Hoboken, N.J., Wiley-Interscience, 455 p.

Krantz, D.E., 2009, A hydrogeomorphic map of Assateague Island National Seashore, Maryland and Virginia, accessed January 11, 2012, at http://www.eeescience.utoledo.edu/ Faculty/Krantz/download_files/NPS_Report.Assateague_Hydrogeomorphology.pdf.

Krantz, D.E., Schupp, C.A., Spaur, Thomas, J.E., and Wells, D.V., 2009, Dynamic systems at the land-sea interface, in Dennison, W.C., Thomas, J.E., Cain, C.J., Carruthers, T.J.B., Hall, M.R., Jesien, R.V., Wazniak, C.E., and Wilson, D.E., eds., Shifting sands—Environmental and cultural change in Maryland's coastal bays: Cambridge, Md., IAN Press, University of Maryland Center for Environmental Science, p. 211–248.

Konikow, L.F., and Reilly, T.E., 1999, Groundwater modeling, in Delleur, J.W., ed., The handbook of groundwater engineering: Boca Raton, Fla., CRC Press, 40 p.

Langevin, C.D., Thorne, D.T., Jr., Dausman, A.M., Sukop, M.C., and Guo, Weixing, 2007, SEAWAT version 4: A computer program for simulation of multi-species solute and heat transport: U.S. Geological Survey Techniques and Methods, book 6, chap. A22, 39 p.

Masterson, J.P., and Garabedian, S.P., 2007, Effects of sea-level rise on ground water flow in a coastal aquifer system: Ground Water, v. 45, no. 2, p. 209–217.

McDonald, M.G., and Harbaugh, A.W., 1988, A modular three-dimensional finite-difference ground-water flow model: U.S. Geological Survey Techniques of Water-Resources Investigations, book 6, chap. A1, 586 p.

Milly, P.C.D., 1994, Climate, soil-water storage, and the average annual water balance: Water Resources Research, v. 30, no. 7, p. 2143–2156.

Morton, R.A., Bracone, J.E., and Cooke, Brian, 2007, The geomorphology and depositional sub-environments of Assateague Island MD/VA: U.S. Geological Survey Open-File Report 2007–1388, CD–ROM, http://pubs.usgs.gov/of/2007/1388/start.html.

Mulligan, A.E., Langevin, C.D., and Post, V.E., 2011, Tidal boundary conditions in SEAWAT: Ground Water, v. 49, no. 6, p. 866–879.

National Oceanic and Atmospheric Administration, 2010a, NCDC Climate-Radar Data Inventories, accessed August 9, 2010, at http://www4.ncdc.noaa.gov/cgi-win/wwcgi.dll?wwDI~StrnSrch~20009427.

National Oceanic and Atmospheric Administration, 2010b, Center for Oceanographic Products and Services, tides and currents information, accessed December 5, 2010, at http://tidesandcurrents.noaa.gov/index.shtml.

Nayegandhi, Amar, Brock, J.C., and Wright, C.W., 2009, Small-footprint, waveform-resolving lidar estimation of submerged and sub-canopy topography in coastal environments: International Journal of Remote Sensing, v. 30, no. 4, p. 861–878.

Nielsen, Peter, 1999, Groundwater dynamics and salinity in coastal barriers: Journal of Coastal Research, v. 15, no. 3, p. 732–740.

Nielsen, Peter, and Hanslow, D.J., 1991, Wave runup distributions on natural beaches: Journal of Coastal Research, v. 7, no. 4, p. 1139–1152.

Owens, J.P., and Denny, C.S., 1979, Upper Cenozoic deposits of the central Delmarva Peninsula: U.S. Geological Survey Professional Paper, 1067–A, 28 p.

Parker, B.B., Hess, K.W., Milbert, D.G., and Gill, S.K., 2003. A national vertical datum transformation tool: Sea Technology, v. 44, no. 9, p. 10–15.

Pendleton, E.A., Williams, S.J., and Thieler, E.R., 2004, Coastal vulnerability assessment of Assateague Island National Seashore (ASIS) to sea-level rise: U.S. Geological Survey Open-File Report 2004–1020, 20 p.

Reilly, T.E., 2001, System and boundary conceptualization in groundwater flow simulation: U.S. Geological Survey Techniques of Water-Resources Investigations, book 3, chap. B8, 38 p.

Rubin, Y., 2003, Applied stochastic hydrogeology: New York, Oxford University Press, 391 p.

Sanford, W.E., Pope, J.P., Selnick, D.L., and Stumvoll, R.F., 2012, Simulation of groundwater flow in the shallow aquifer system of the Delmarva Peninsula, Maryland and Delaware: U.S. Geological Survey Open-File Report 2012–1140, 58 p.

Sanford, W.E., Pope, J.P., and Nelms, D.L., 2009, Simulation of groundwater-level and salinity changes in the Eastern Shore, Virginia: U.S. Geological Survey Scientific Investigations Report 2009–5066, 125 p.

Schubert, C.E., 2010, Analysis of the shallow groundwater flow system at Fire Island National Seashore, Suffolk County, New York: U.S. Geological Survey Scientific Investigations Report 2009–5259, 106 p.

Trapp, Henry, Jr., 1997, GROUND WATER ATLAS of the UNITED STATES—Delaware, Maryland, New Jersey, North Carolina, Pennsylvania, Virginia, West Virginia: U.S. Geological Survey Hydrologic Investigations Atlas 730–L, 124 p.

Wells, D.V., and Conkwright, R.D., 1999, Maryland coastal bays sediment mapping project—The physical and chemical characteristics of the shallow sediments—Atlas and synthesis report: Coastal and Estuarine Geology Program File Report 99–5, Maryland Department of Natural Resosurces, Maryland Geological Survey, Baltimore, Maryland.

Werner, A.D., and Simmons, C.T., 2009, Impact of sea-level rise on sea water intrusion in coastal aquifers: Ground Water, v. 47, no. 2, p. 197–204.

Williams, J.H., Lapham, W.W., and Barringer, T.H., 1993, Application of electromagnetic logging to contamination investigations in glacial sand-and-gravel aquifers: Ground Water Monitoring and Remediation, v. 13, no. 3, p. 129–138.

Zheng, Chunmiao, and Wang, P.P., 1999, MT3DMS—A modular three-dimensional multispecies transport model for simulation of advection, dispersion, and chemical reactions of contaminants in groundwater systems—Documentation and user's guide: U.S. Army Corps of Engineers Contract Report SEDRP–99–1, 169 p.

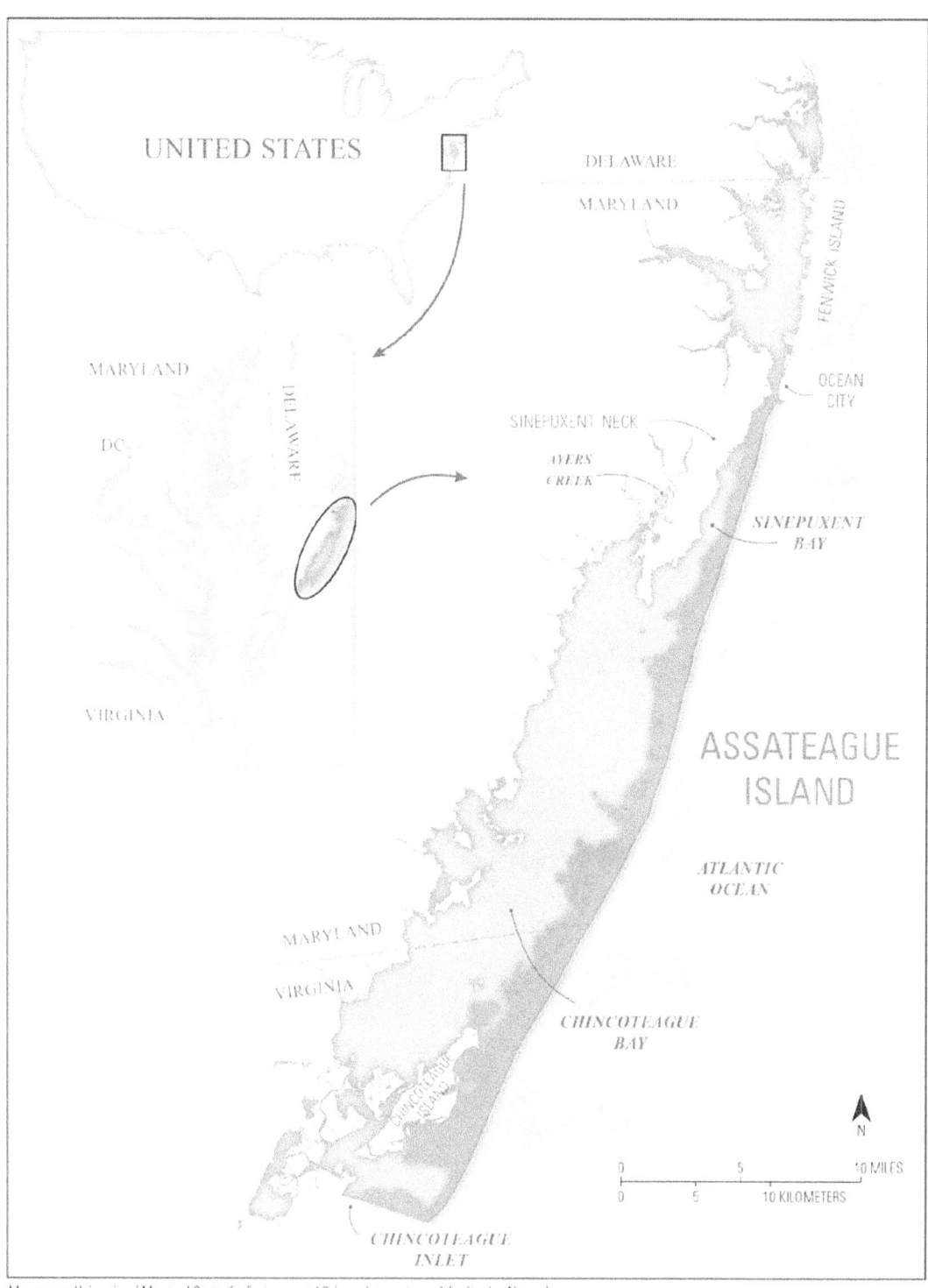

Map source: University of Maryland Center for Environmental Science-Integration and Application Network

Figure 1. Map showing the location of Assateague Island, Maryland and Virginia. Figure used with the permission of the University of Maryland Center for Environmental Science-Integration and Application Network.

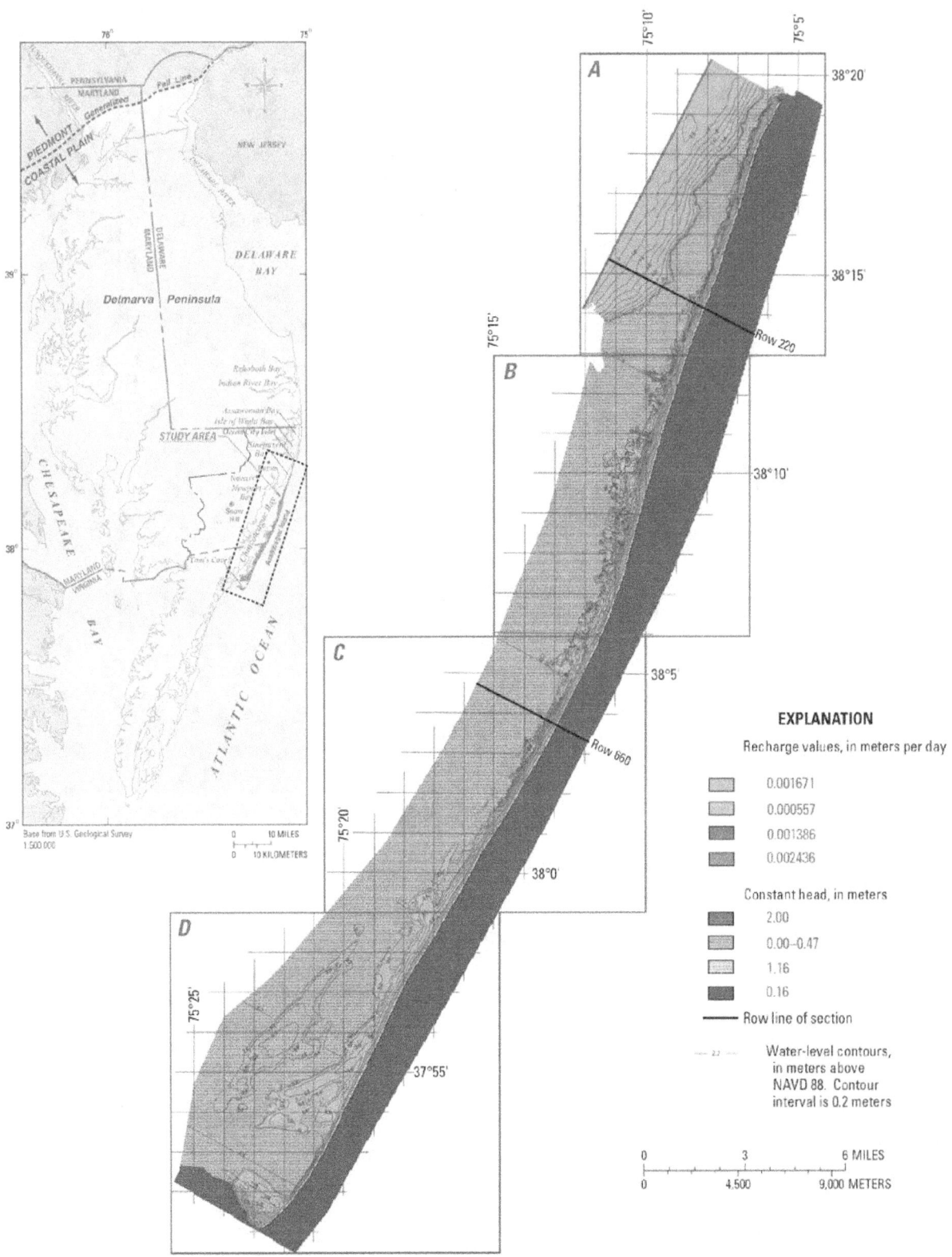

Figure 2. Map showing study area and the model grid extent with zones A through D and lines of section, Assateague Island, Maryland and Virginia. (Cross sections are shown in figure 3.)

EXPLANATION

Recharge values, in meters per day

- 0.001671
- 0.000557
- 0.001386
- 0.002436

Constant head, in meters

- 2.00
- 0.00–0.47
- 1.16
- 0.16

— Row line of section

Water-level contours, in meters above NAVD 88. Contour interval is 0.2 meters

16

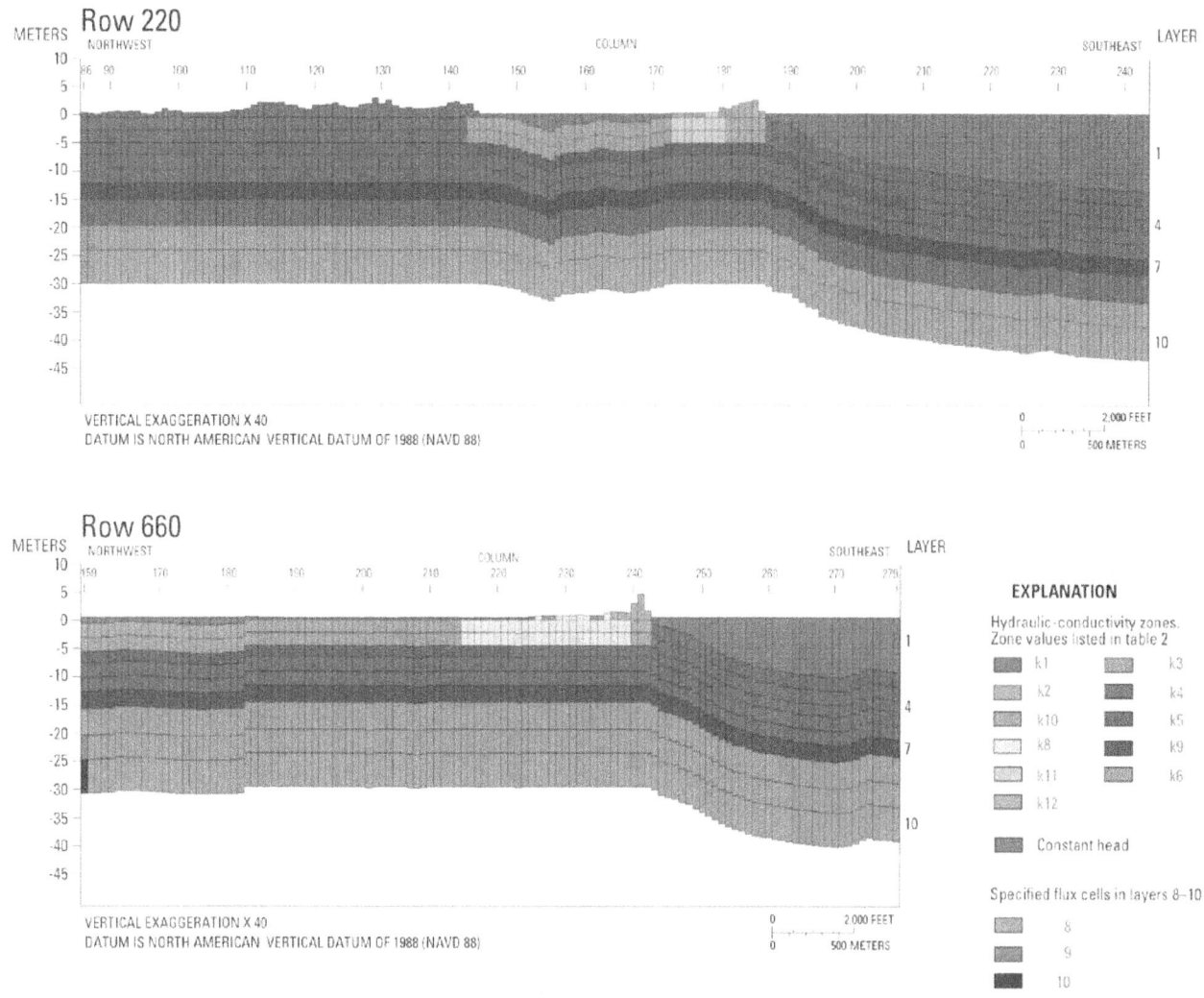

Figure 3. Sections showing vertical layering and distribution of hydraulic conductivity zones in the numerical model of Assateague Island, Maryland and Virginia. (Section lines are shown in figure 2.)

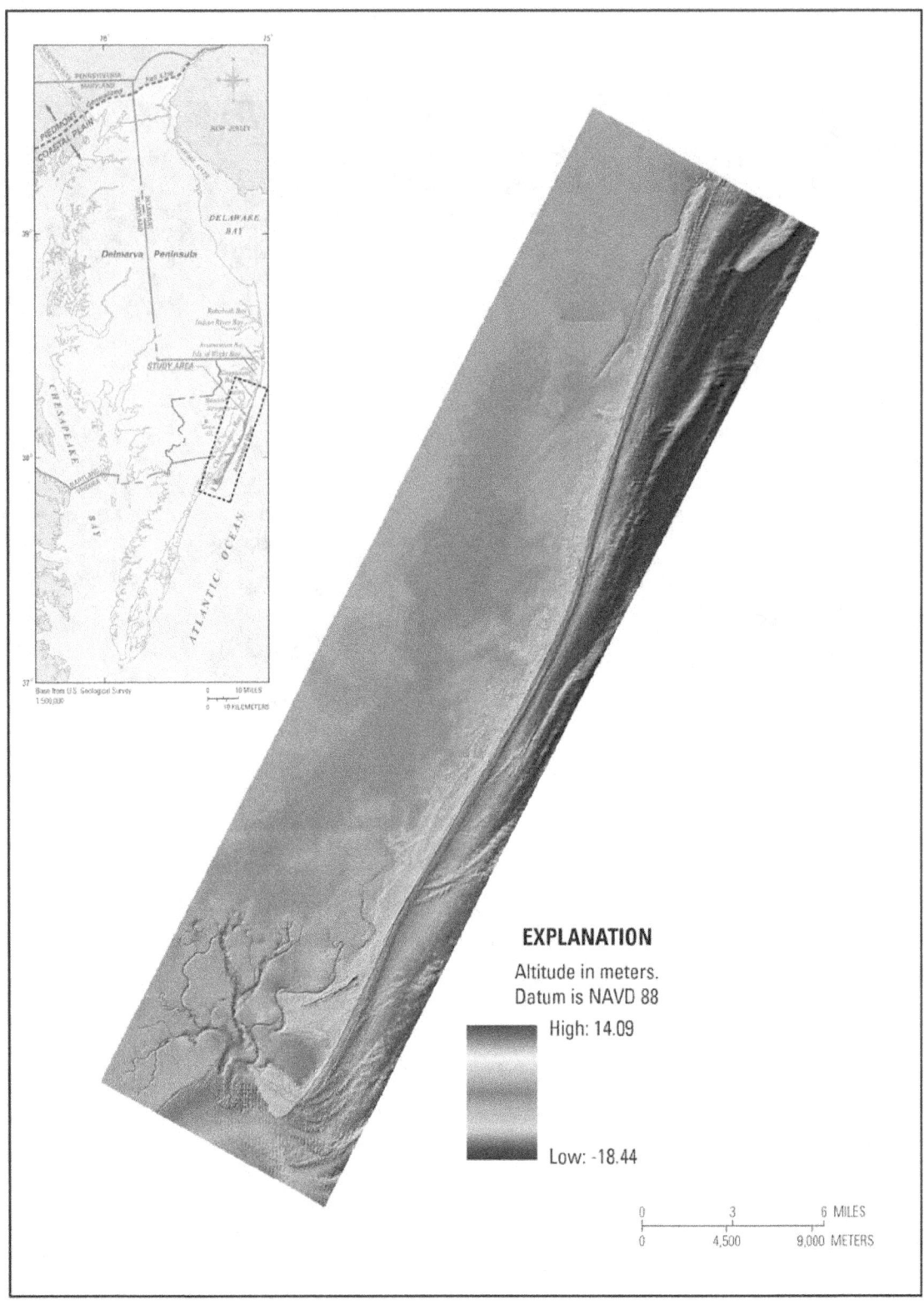

Figure 4. Map showing the spatially variable topographic and bathymetric surfaces used in the development of the numerical model of Assateague Island, Maryland and Virginia.

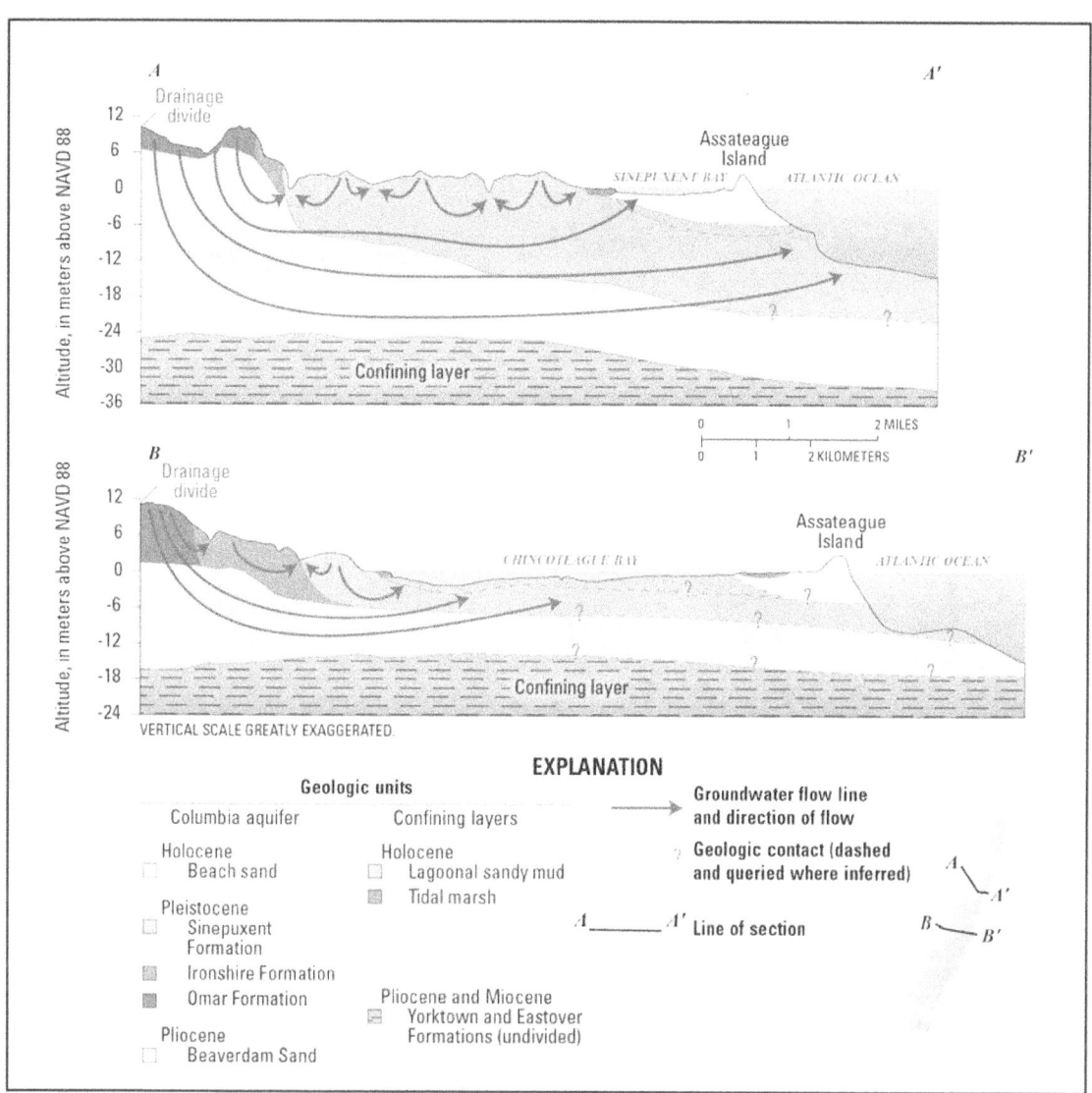

Figure 5. Schematic sections showing the hydrogeologic framework beneath Assateague Island, Maryland and Virginia. Modified from Krantz and others (2009).

19

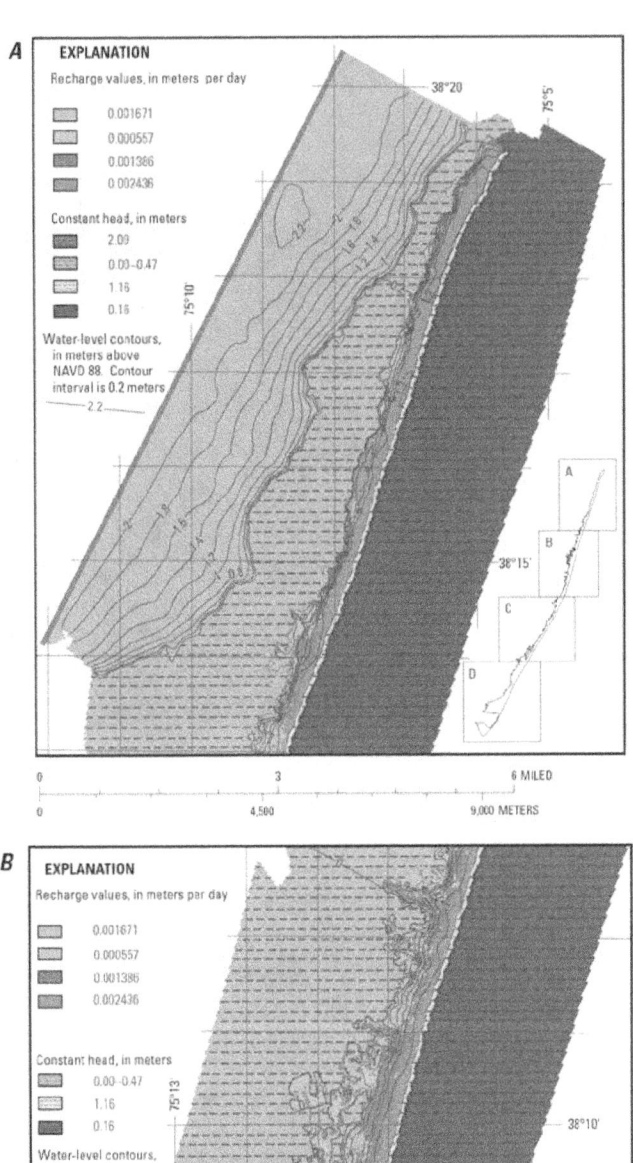

Figure 6. Maps showing distribution of recharge and constant-head boundaries and the water-level contours simulated for zones A through D in the numerical model of Assateague Island, Maryland and Virginia.

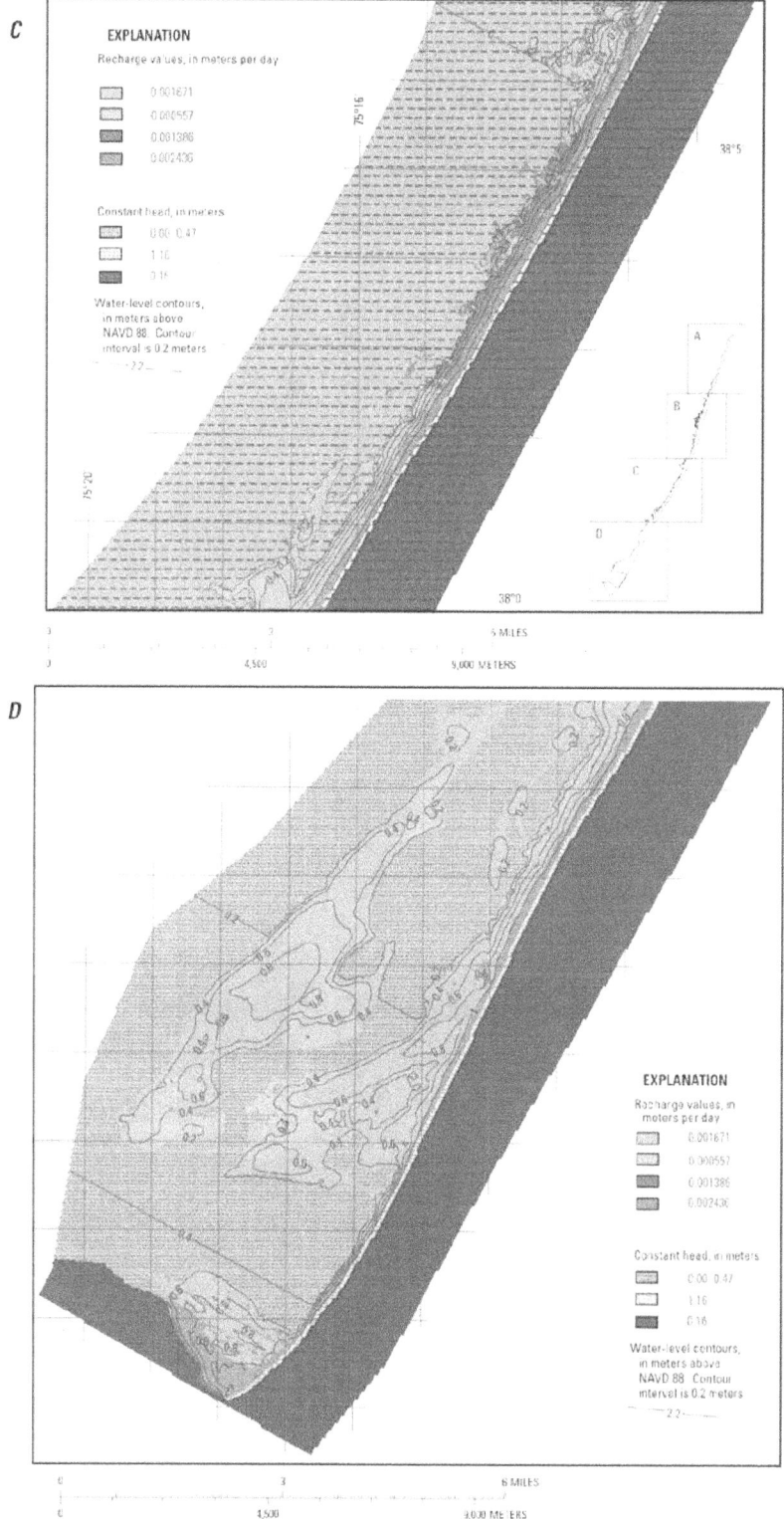

Figure 6. Maps showing distribution of recharge and constant-head boundaries and the water-level contours simulated for zones A through D in the numerical model of Assateague Island, Maryland and Virginia.—Continued

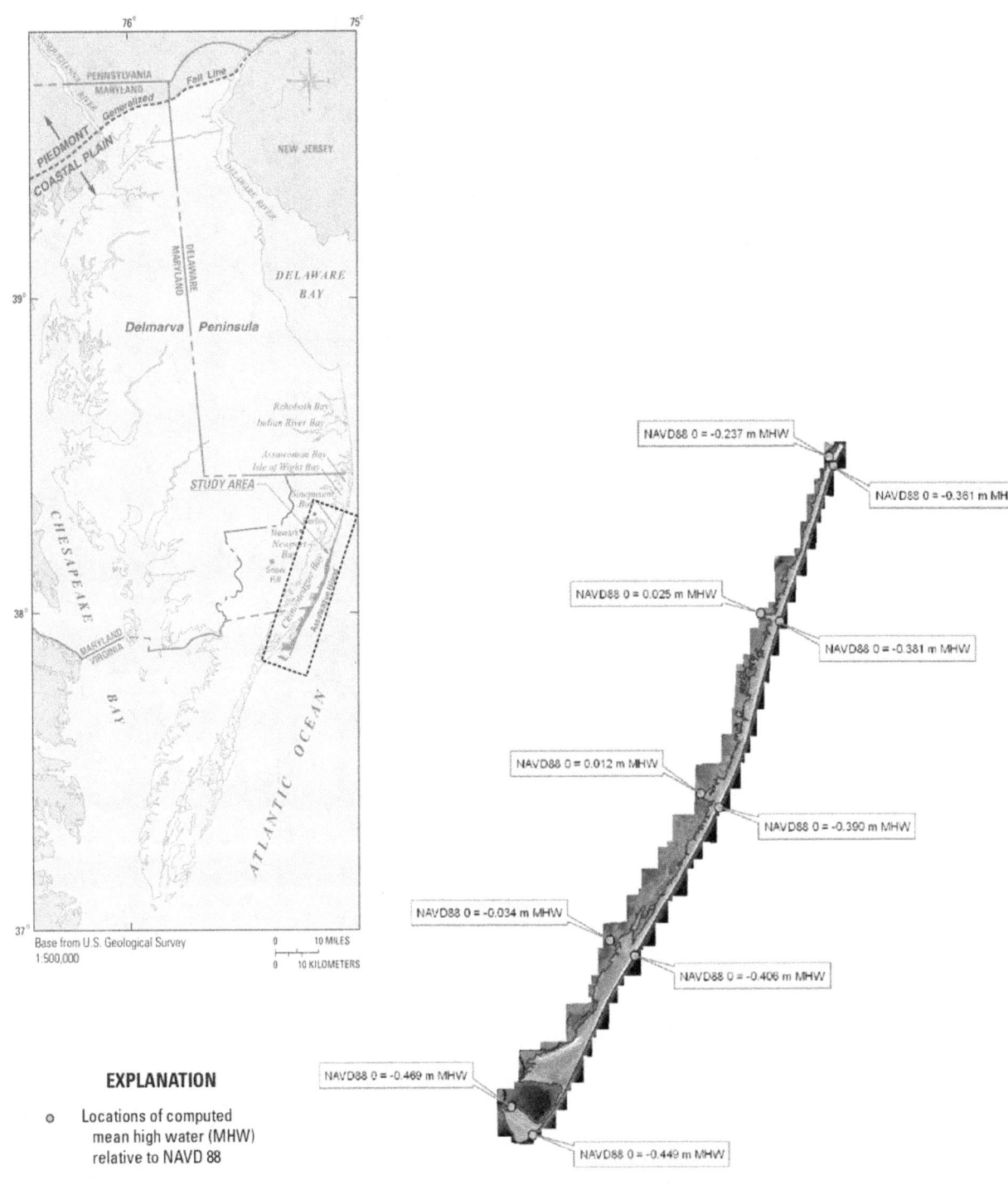

Figure 7. Map showing distribution of mean high-water altitudes calculated by using VDatum for Assateague Island, Maryland and Virginia. (m, meter; MHW, mean high water)

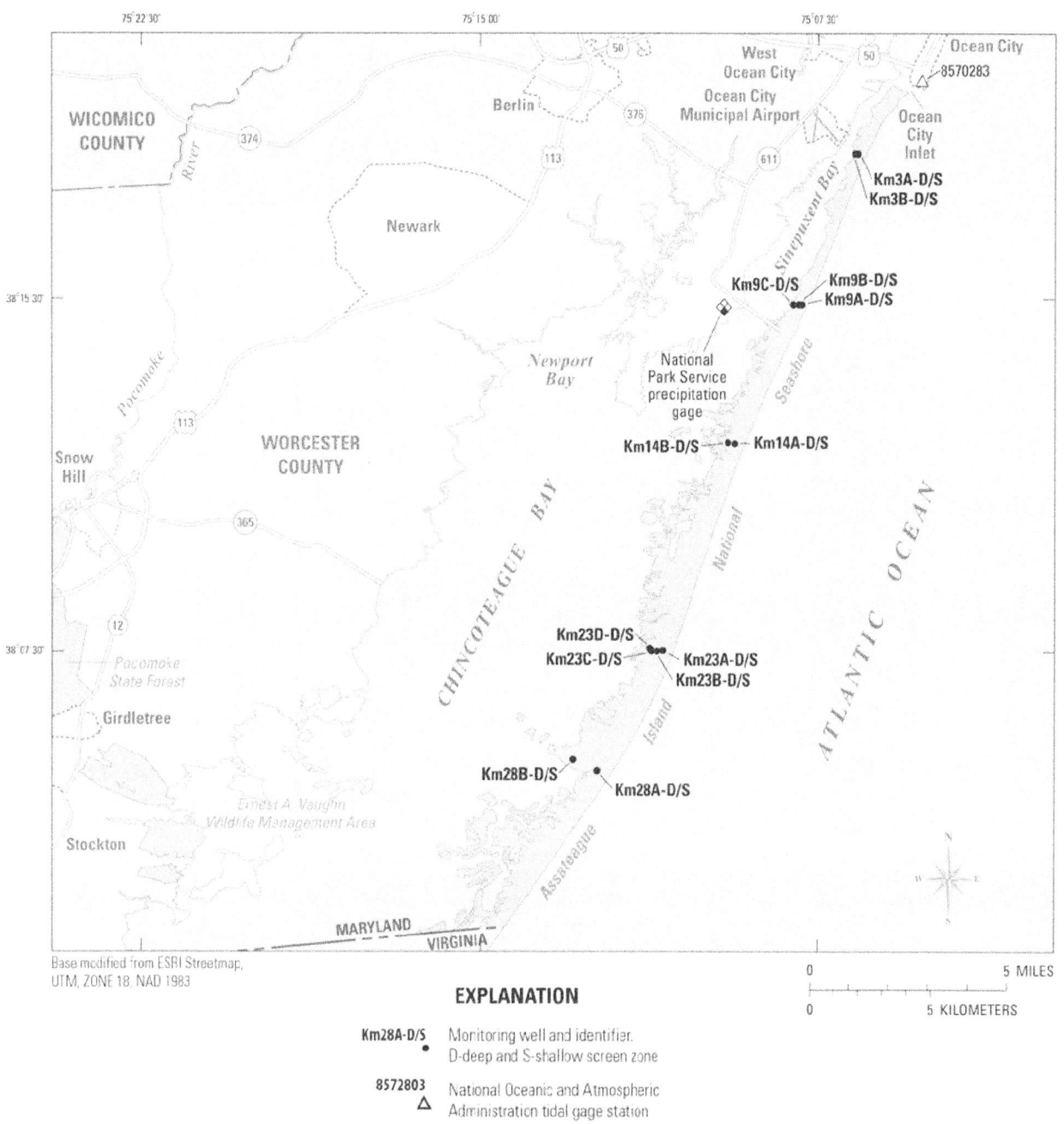

Figure 8. Map showing monitoring-well locations along five transects, Assateague Island, Maryland and Virginia (from Banks and others, 2012).

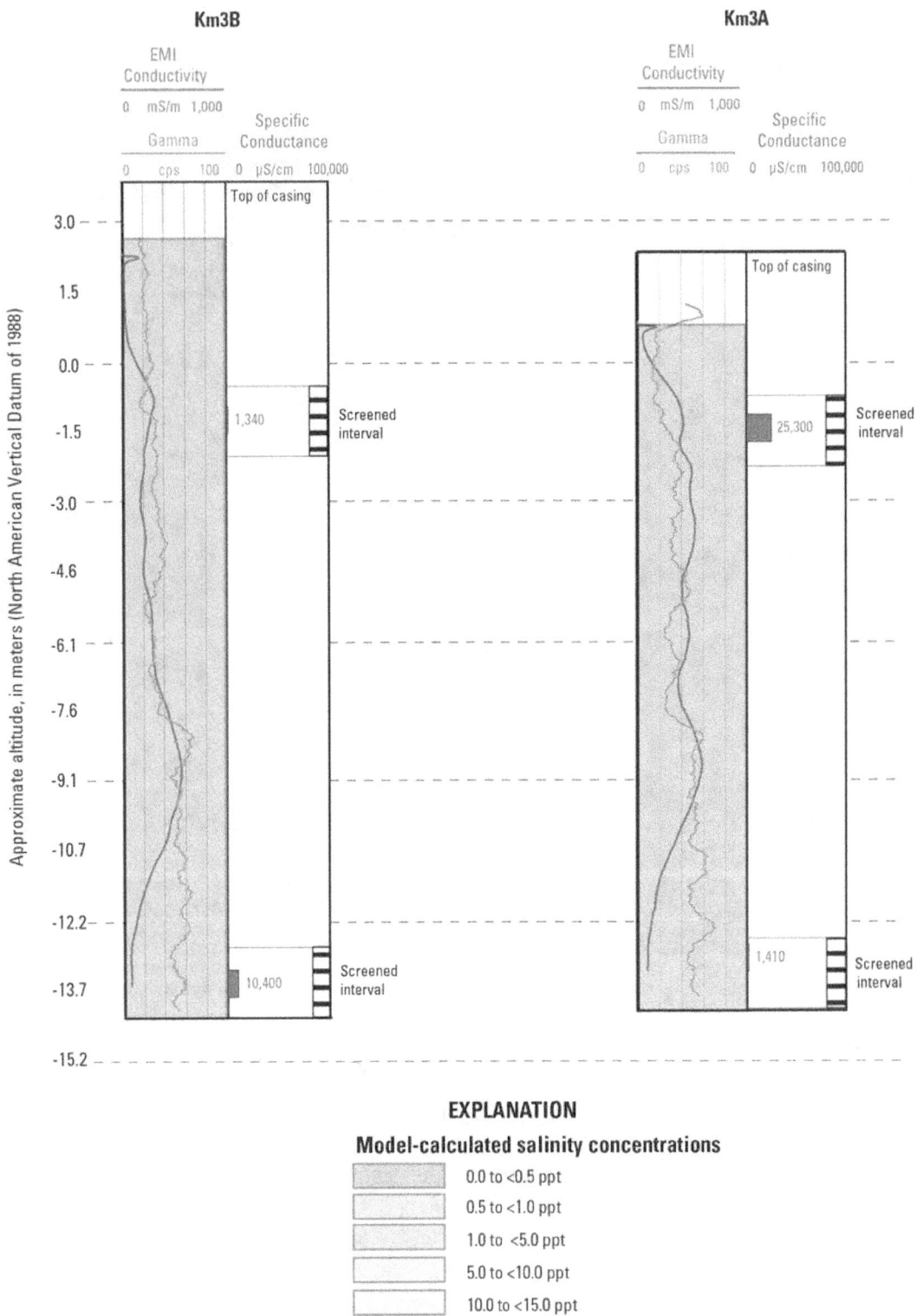

Figure 9. Plots showing selected monitoring wells with model-calculated salinity concentrations in parts per thousand, specific conductance, and electromagnetic induction logs, Assateague Island, Maryland and Virginia, October 2010 (modified from Banks and others, 2012).

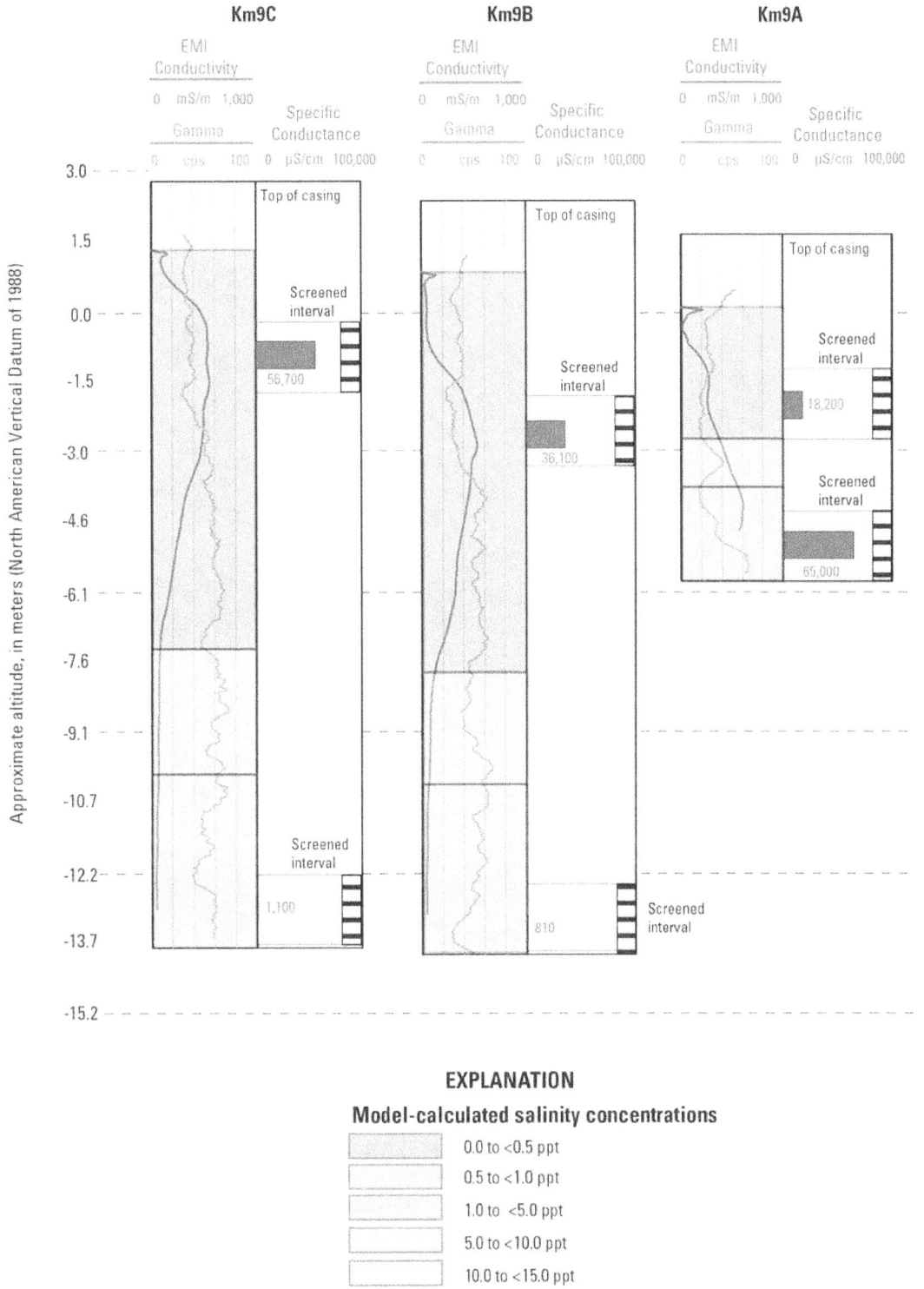

Figure 9. Plots showing selected monitoring wells with model-calculated salinity concentrations in parts per thousand, specific conductance, and electromagnetic induction logs, Assateague Island, Maryland and Virginia, October 2010 (modified from Banks and others, 2012).—Continued

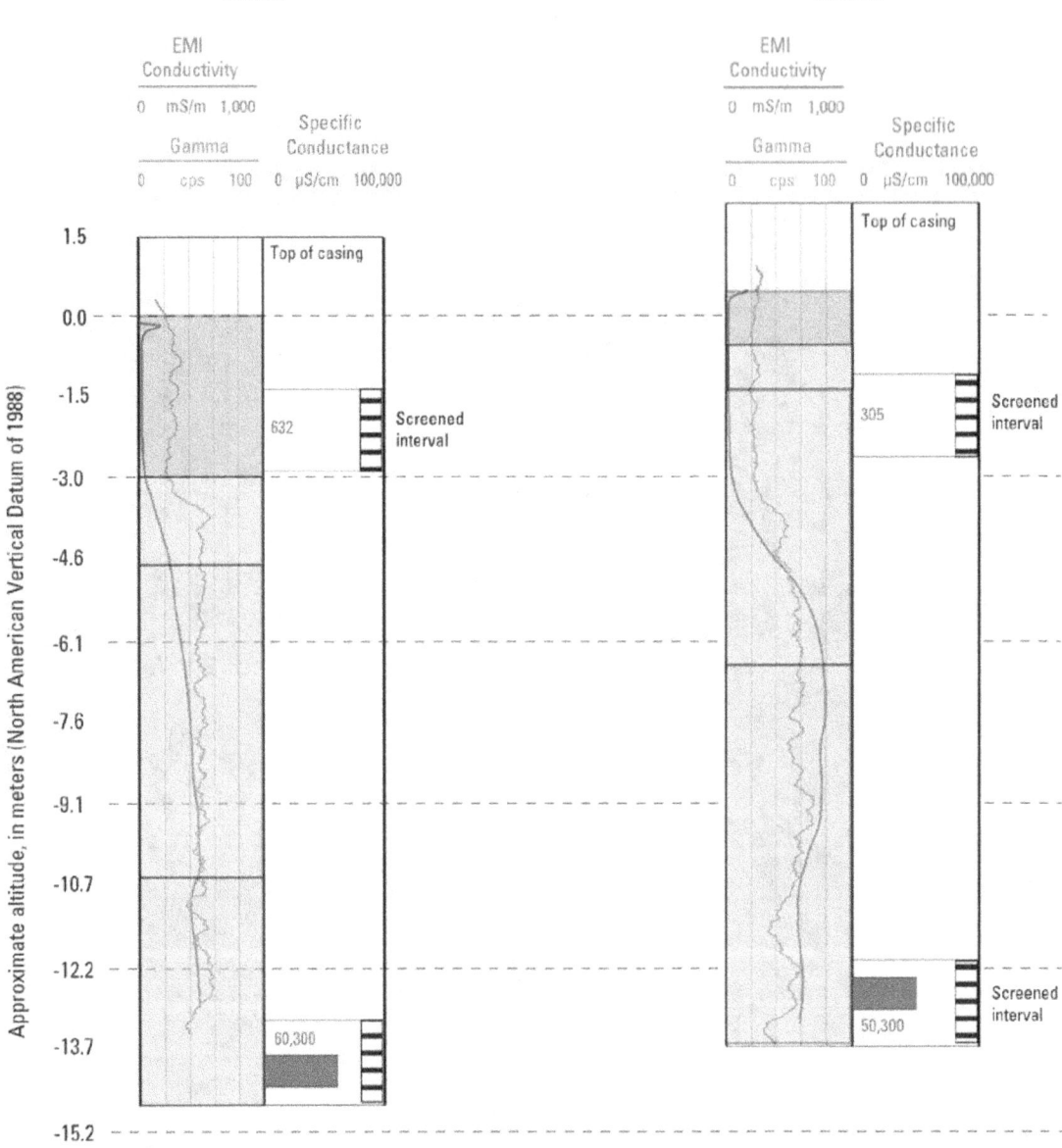

Figure 9. Plots showing selected monitoring wells with model-calculated salinity concentrations in parts per thousand, specific conductance, and electromagnetic induction logs, Assateague Island, Maryland and Virginia, October 2010 (modified from Banks and others, 2012).—Continued

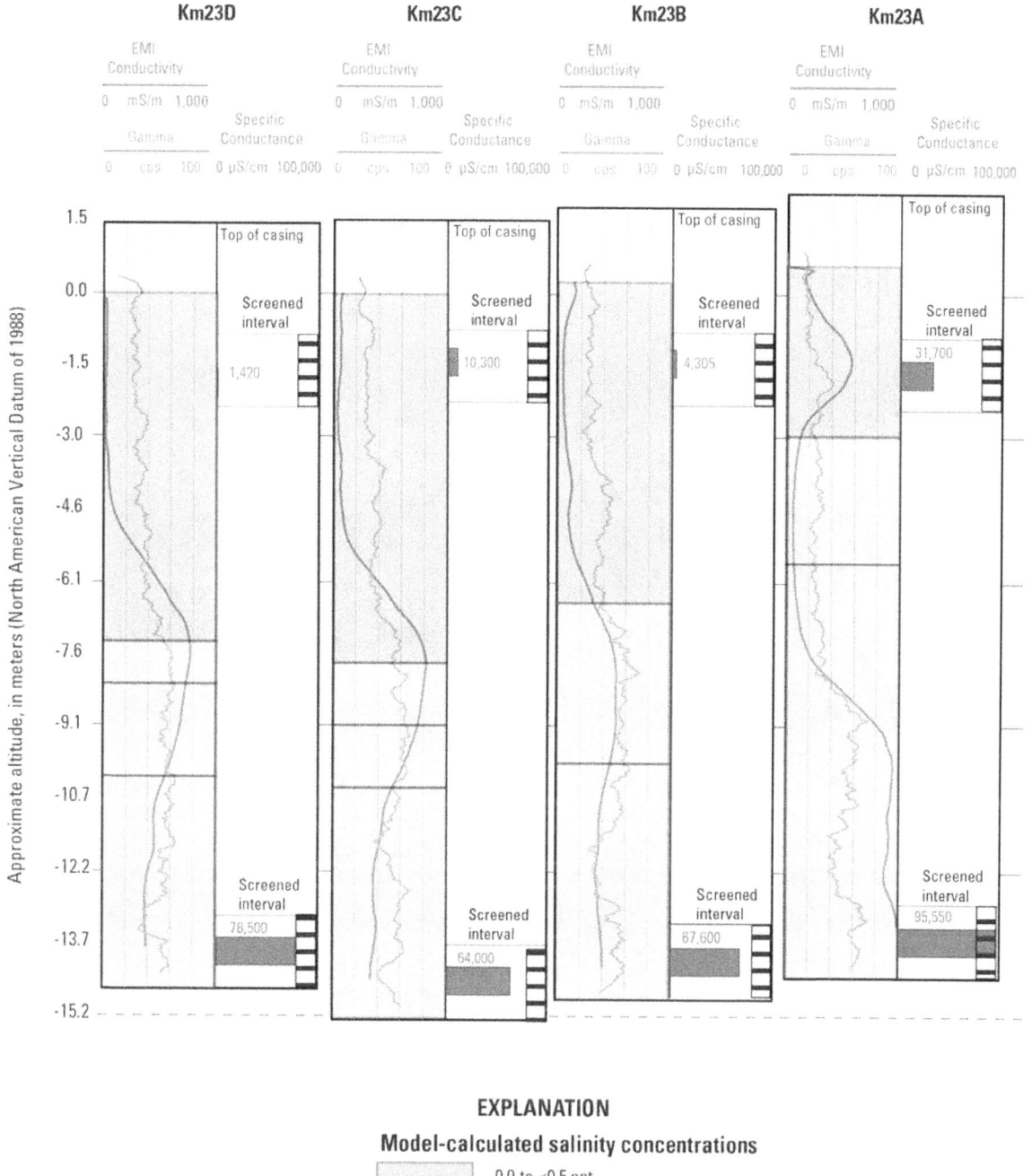

Figure 9. Plots showing selected monitoring wells with model-calculated salinity concentrations in parts per thousand, specific conductance, and electromagnetic induction logs, Assateague Island, Maryland and Virginia, October 2010 (modified from Banks and others, 2012).—Continued

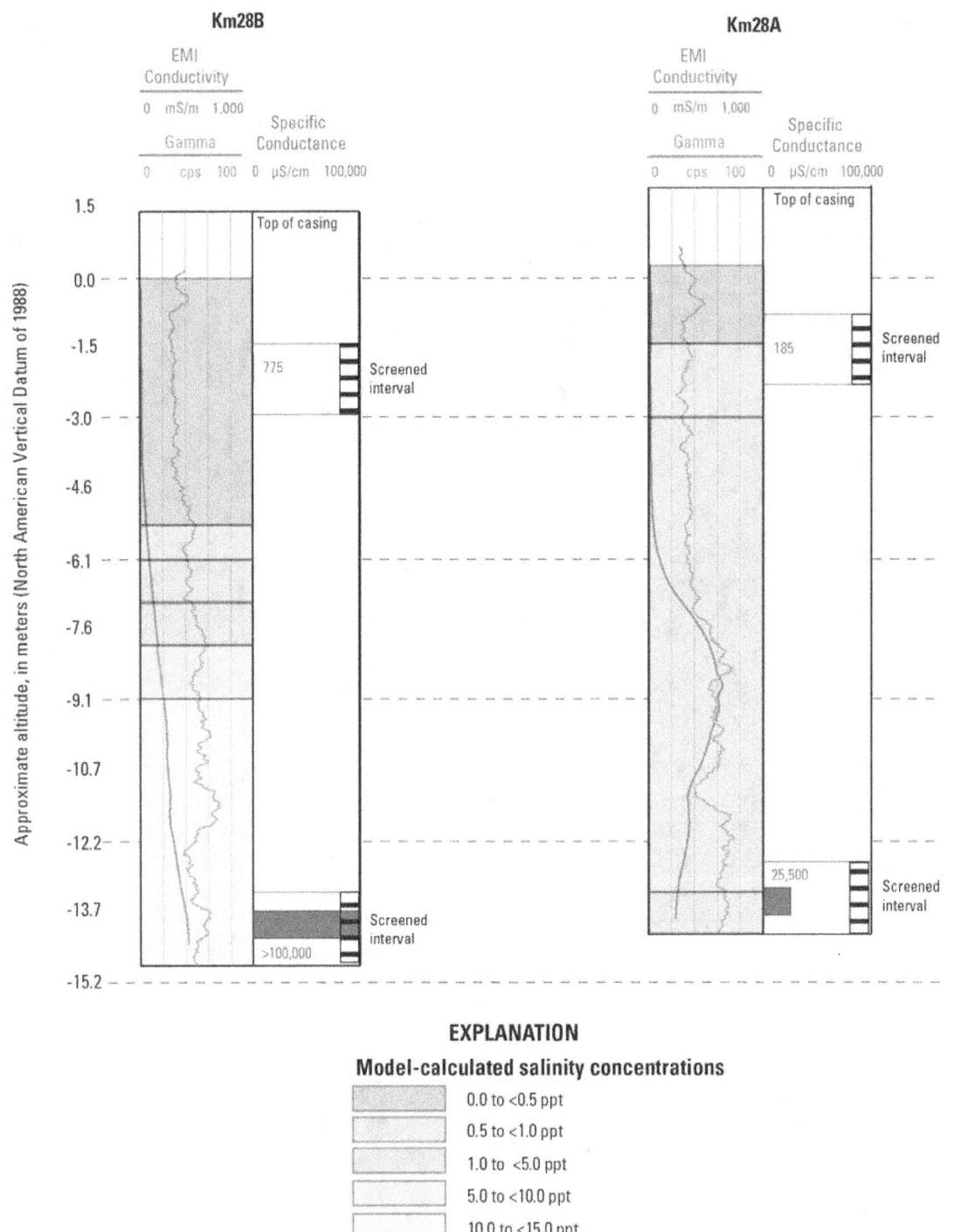

Figure 9. Plots showing selected monitoring wells with model-calculated salinity concentrations in parts per thousand, specific conductance, and electromagnetic induction logs, Assateague Island, Maryland and Virginia, October 2010 (modified from Banks and others, 2012).—Continued

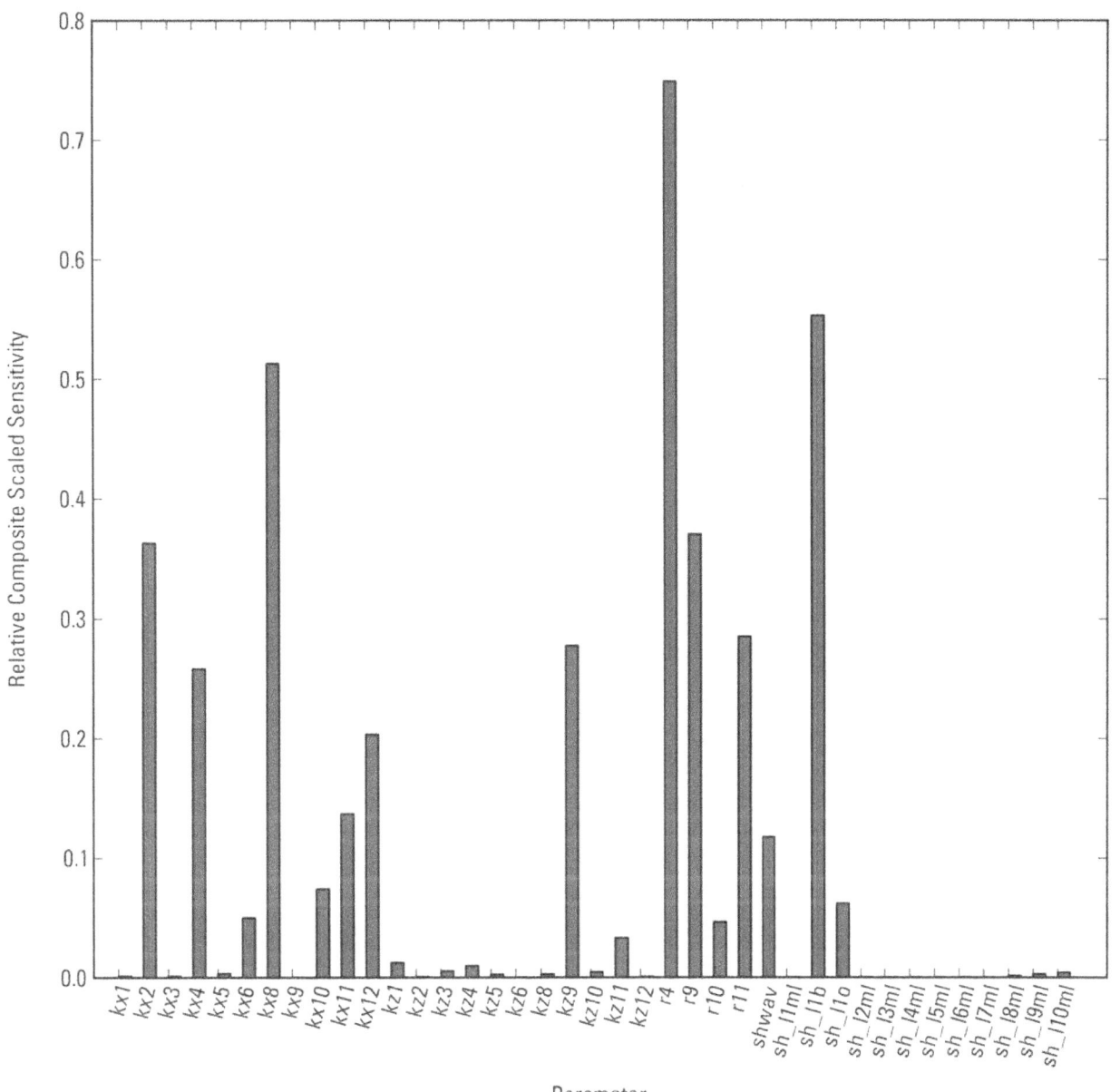

Figure 10. Graph showing relative composite-scaled sensitivity values evaluated at the initial parameter values. The "kx and kz" parameters indicate horizontal and vertical hydraulic conductivity values for zones 1–12. The "r" indicates recharge for zones 4, 9, 10, and 11, "sh_lml" indicates mainland constant head in layers 1–10, "shwav" is the constant head in the beach zone, "sh_l1b" is the constant head along Sinepuxent Bay, and "sh_l1o" is the starting head on the ocean boundary.

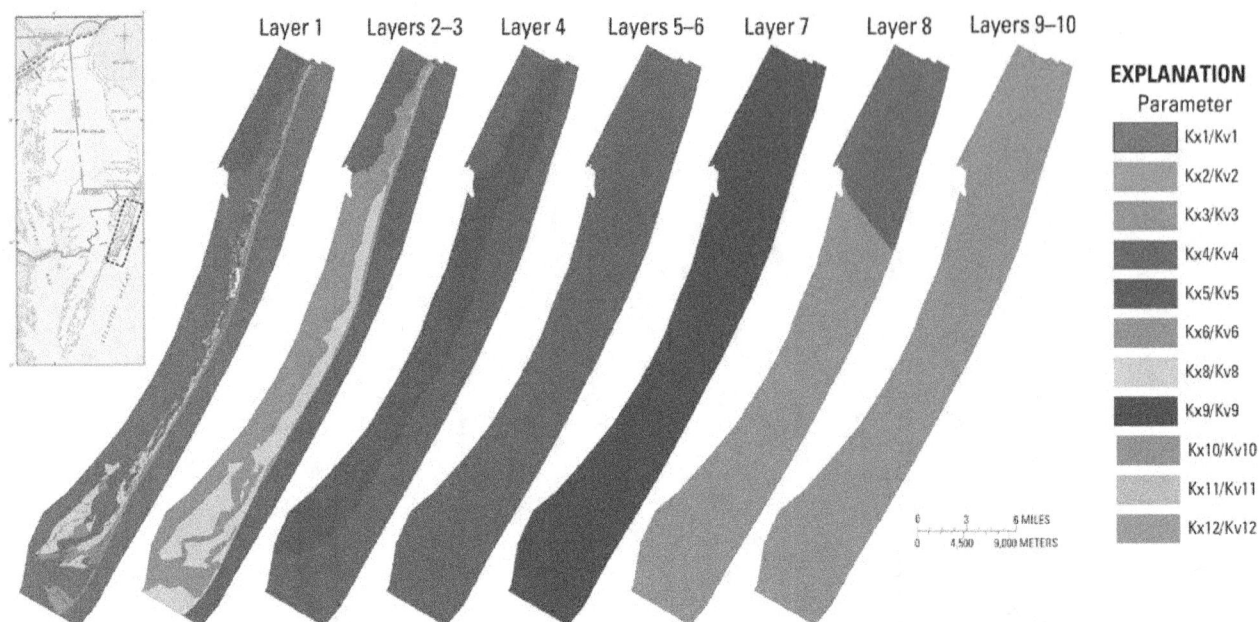

Figure 11. Map showing hydraulic conductivity zonation in the 10 layers of the groundwater-flow model of Assateague Island, Maryland and Virginia. (Initial and optimal hydraulic conductivity values are listed in table 2).

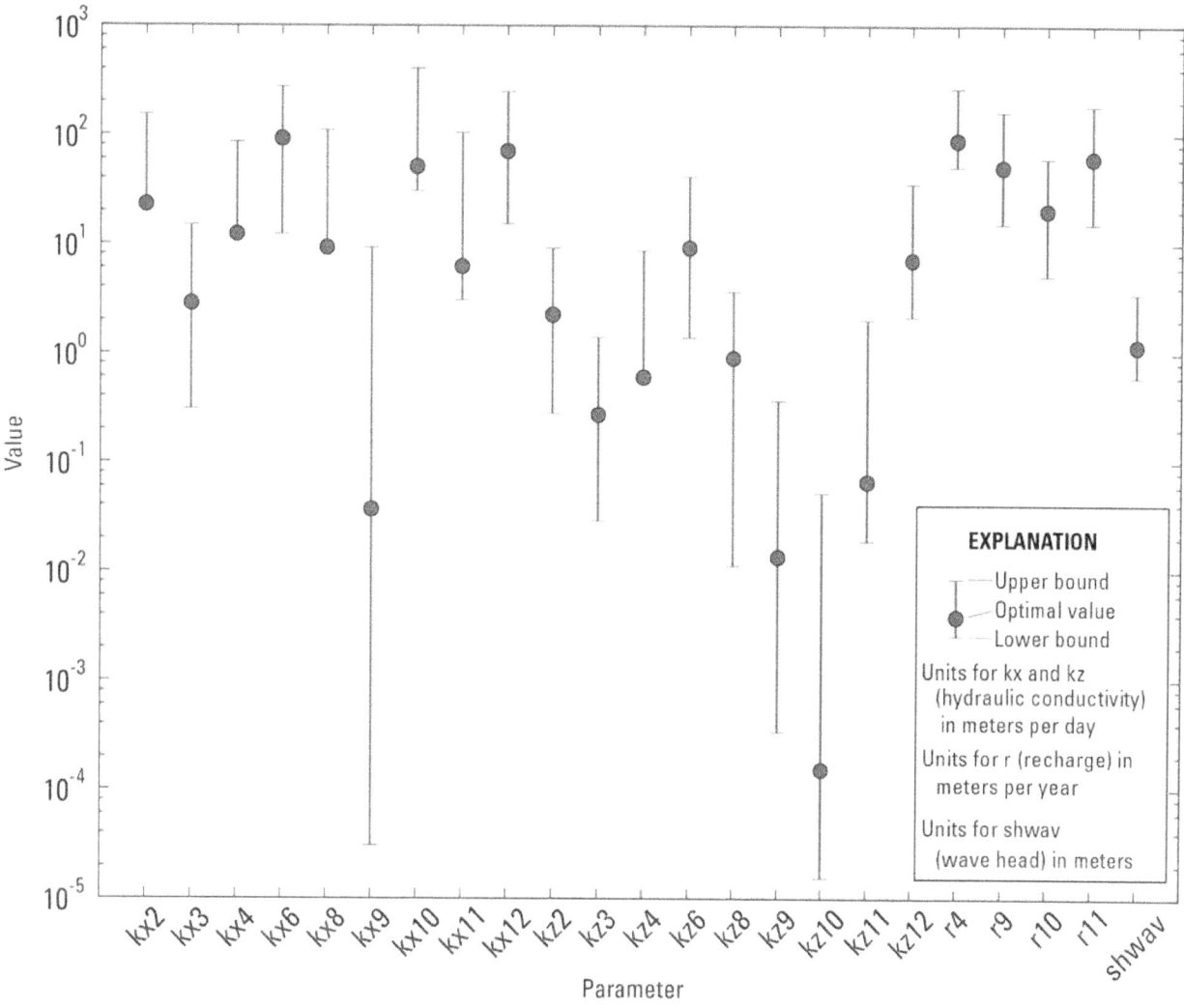

Figure 12. Plot showing the range and final optimal values of the parameters used in the groundwater-flow model of Assateague Island, Maryland and Virginia.

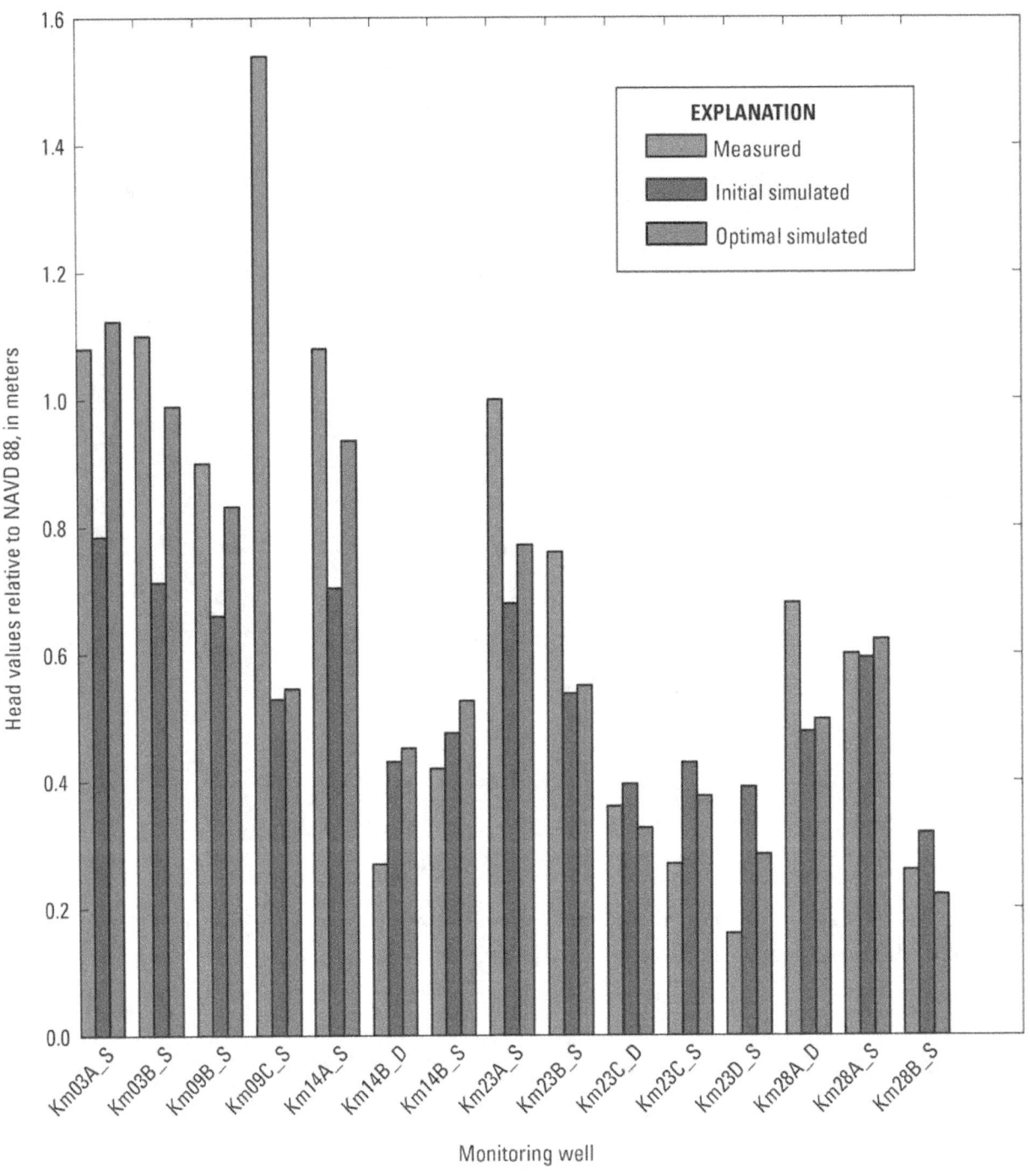

Figure 13. Graph showing the measured, initial simulated, and final simulated head values for the monitoring wells used as calibration data, Assateague Island, Maryland and Virginia.

Table 1. Measured and simulated heads, epistemic uncertainty, and weight for selected wells used to calibrate the groundwater-flow model, Assateague Island, Maryland and Virginia.

[Heads are in meters(m), referenced to NAVD 88. USGS ID, U.S. Geological Survey identifier; n/a, not applicable]

Monitoring well	USGS ID	Measured head (m)	Epistemic uncertainty (m)	Weight	Initial simulated head (m)	Optimal simulated head (m)
Km03A_S	381804075063402	1.08	0.10	10.00	0.78	1.12
Km03B_S	381805075063502	1.10	0.10	10.00	0.71	1.00
Km09B_S	381452075075902	0.90	0.10	10.00	0.66	0.82
Km09C_S	381452075080102	1.54	n/a	0.00	0.53	0.53
Km14A_S	381155075091802	1.08	0.10	10.00	0.70	0.91
Km14B_D	381157075092901	0.27	n/a	0.00	0.43	0.44
Km14B_S	381157075092902	0.42	0.10	10.00	0.48	0.52
Km23A_S	380731075105602	1.00	0.10	10.00	0.68	0.77
Km23B_S	380730075110402	0.76	0.10	10.00	0.54	0.54
Km23C_D	380731075111101	0.36	n/a	0.00	0.40	0.32
Km23C_S	380731075111102	0.27	0.10	10.00	0.43	0.38
Km23D_S	380734075111302	0.16	0.10	10.00	0.39	0.29
Km28A_D	380457075122301	0.68	n/a	0.00	0.48	0.50
Km28A_S	380457075122302	0.60	0.02	50.00	0.59	0.63
Km28B_S	380512075125402	0.26	0.02	50.00	0.32	0.22

Table 2. Initial and final optimal parameter values used in the flow model of Assateague Island, Maryland and Virginia.

[m/d, meters per day; cm/yr, centimeter per year; m, meter]

Parameter	Description	Initial value	Optimal value
Horizontal hydraulic conductivity (m/d)			
kx1	ocean	15,000	13,589
kx2	beach-south	75	23
kx3	bay bottom_shallow	3	3
kx4	coastal plain	25	12
kx5	coastal plain-bayside	3	tied to xk5
kx6	coastal plain deep	60	91
kx8	beach-bayside	75	9
kx9	confining unit-deep	1.00E–02	3.67E–02
kx10	wetland	300	51
kx11	beach-bayside-north	10	6
kx12	beach-north	50	71
Vertical hydraulic conductivity (m/d)			
kz1	ocean	4,500	0.24
kz2	beach-south	563	2.25
kz3	bay bottom_shallow	0.90	0.27
kz4	coastal plain	63	0.60
kz5	coastal plain-bayside	0.90	tied to kz4
kz6	coastal plain deep	360	9.15
kz8	beach-bayside	563	0.90
kz9	confining unit-deep	1.00E–05	1.35E–02
kz10	wetland	3.00E–01	1.53E–04
kz11	beach-bayside-north	1	0.07
kz12	beach-north	250	7.09
Recharge (cm/yr)			
r4	unvegetated	61.0	89.0
r9	grass/shrub	20.5	50.6
r10	wetland	10.2	20.3
r11	forest	40.2	61.0
Boundary head (m)			
shwav	wave overheight	8.74E–01	1.16